Coloring book for Kids

Princess

Kara Wise

Copyright © 2020 Kara Wise

All rights reserved.

ISBN: 9798639044229

INTRODUCTION

This coloring book is going to be the one that your kids will always remember.

I do believe our children nowadays spend too much time with virtual entertaining rather than listening to stories, drawing and coloring books. Yes, from time to time letting them watch a Youtube video makes sense because they are happy and you can get some relax, but if we focus on what is really the best for developing their skills, there are no doubts that interactive entertainment should be preferred to the passive one.

I have two kids, six and nine, and I have always had the passion for drawing. My professional career took my talents towards other tasks, but I never stopped exercising and fueling my passion whenever I got free time. Back when they grew up a bit and started to get interested in colors, pens and pencils, I started to draw basic forms, letting them express themselves in the most creative way possible.

This is how this book was born. I am so glad I can share it, making sure boys and girls from all over the world can start learning, drawing, coloring and reading with my models.

The theme of the book is princess world and its magic, a journey among queens, knights, magic animals and much more to discover.

In this book you will find 50 easy pictures to color, many of them having different ways to interact with the final result. Your kids will be able to:
- color the pictures deciding the right match for each section of the drawing
- name the subject as they please, exercising their writing skills
- fill the balloons, letting the characters speaks out loud
- read and learn easy words

I hope you as well as your children will enjoy this book, spending quality time together and feeling proud of the result.

Kara

Summary

- PRINCESS 6
- PRINCESS 7
- CASTLE 8
- BABY PRINCESS 9
- PRINCESS 10
- KING 11
- UNICORN 12
- CARRIAGE 13
- FROG 14
- PRINCESS 15
- QUEEN 16
- KNIGHT JUNIOR 17
- PRINCESS 18
- GUARD 19
- PRINCESS 20
- PRINCESS 21
- CASTLE 22
- PRINCESS 23
- HORSE 24
- FAIRY 25
- MERMAID 26
- BIRDS 27
- WITCHER 29
- PRINCESS 30
- PRINCESS 31
- QUEEN 32
- FAIRY 33

MERMAID	34
QUEEN	35
PRINCESS	36
PRINCESS	37
PRINCESS	38
FAIRY	39
PRINCESS	40
PRINCESS	41
BABY UNICORN	42
PRINCESS WITH DOG	43
PRINCESS WITH BIRD	44
UNICORN	45
PRINCESS	46
PRINCE CAT	47
RAINBOW	48
CASTLE	49
SQUIRRELS	50
QUEEN	51
ROSE	52
PRINCESS	53
DRAGONS	54
PRINCESS	55
CONCLUSION	56

PRINCESS

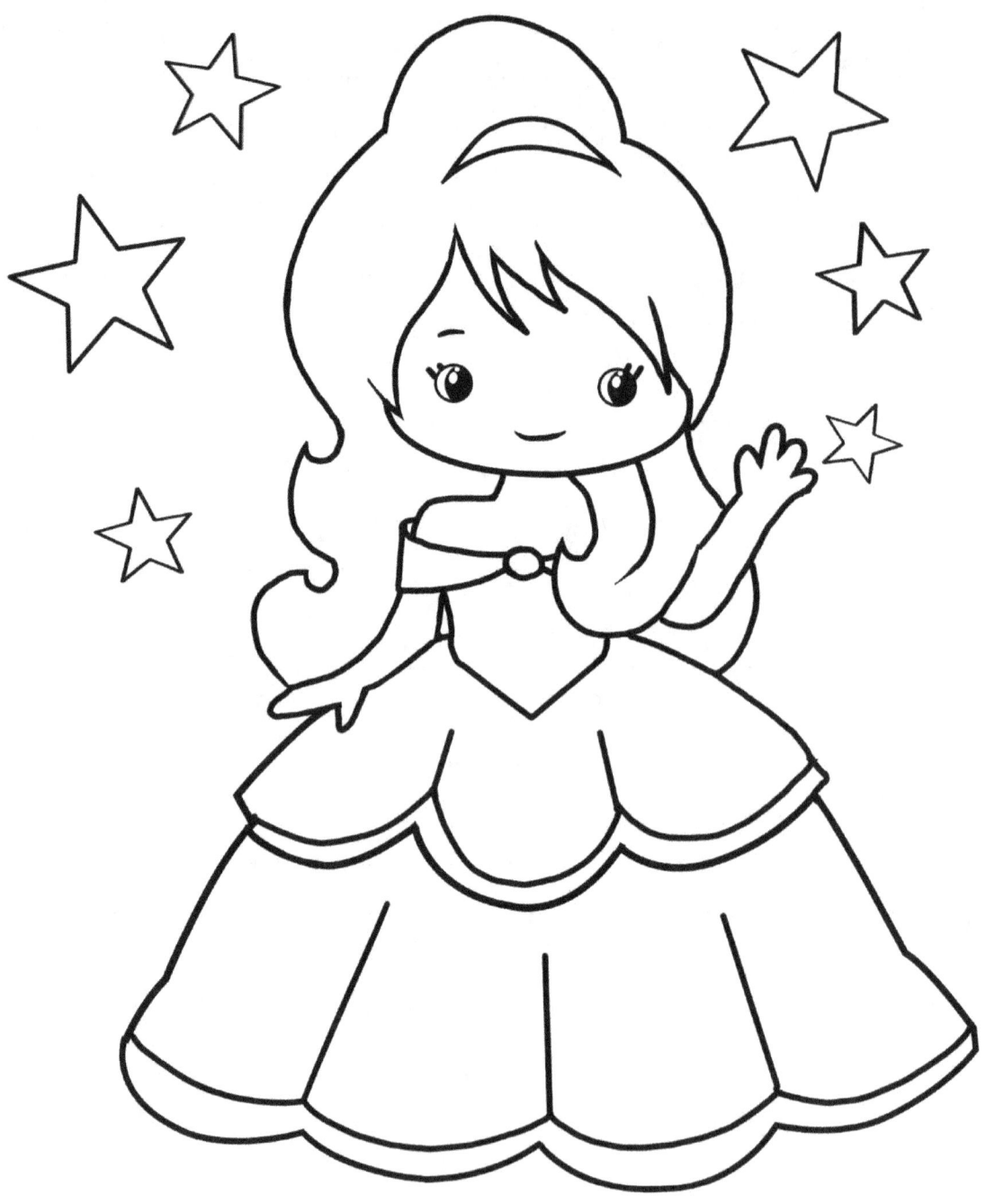

NAME:

PRINCESS

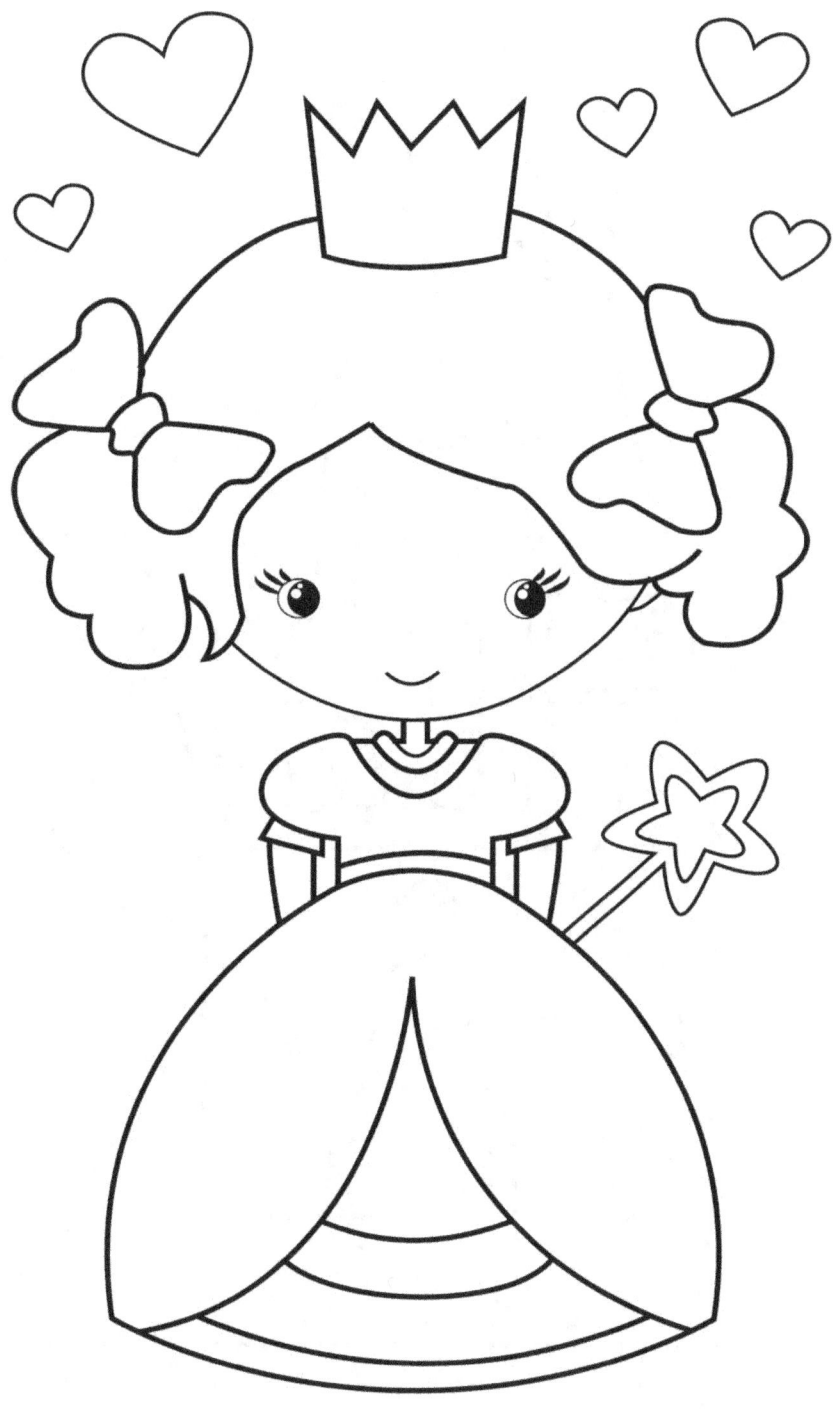

NAME:

CASTLE

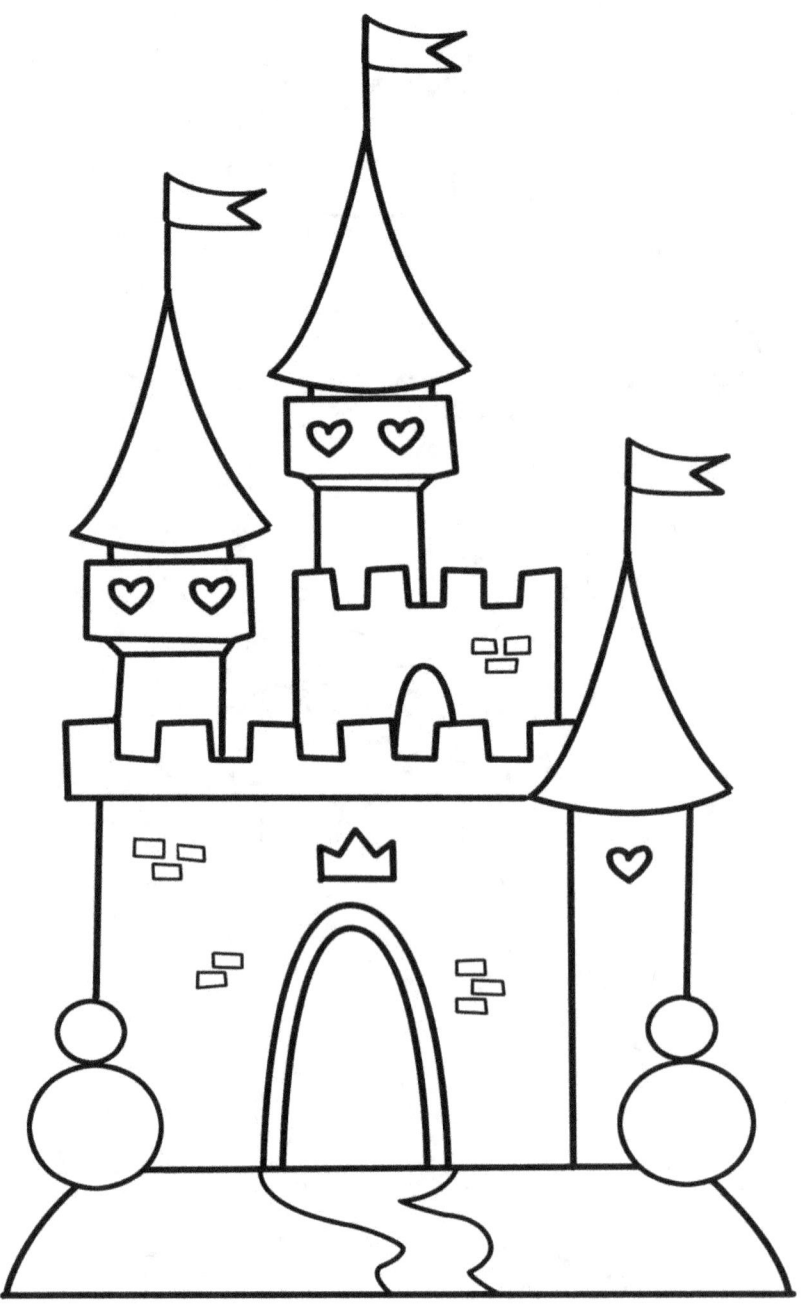

NAME:

BABY PRINCESS

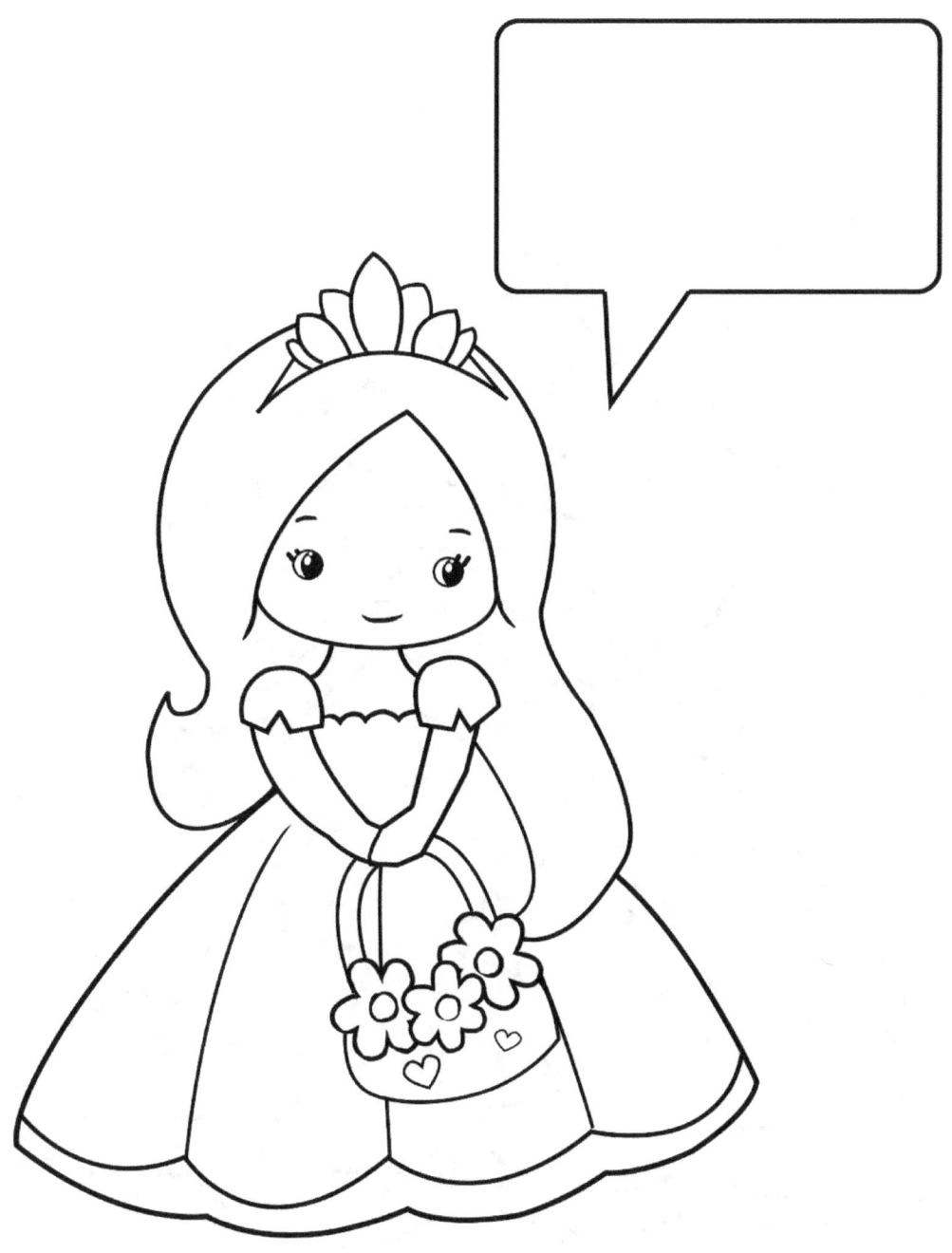

NAME:

PRINCESS

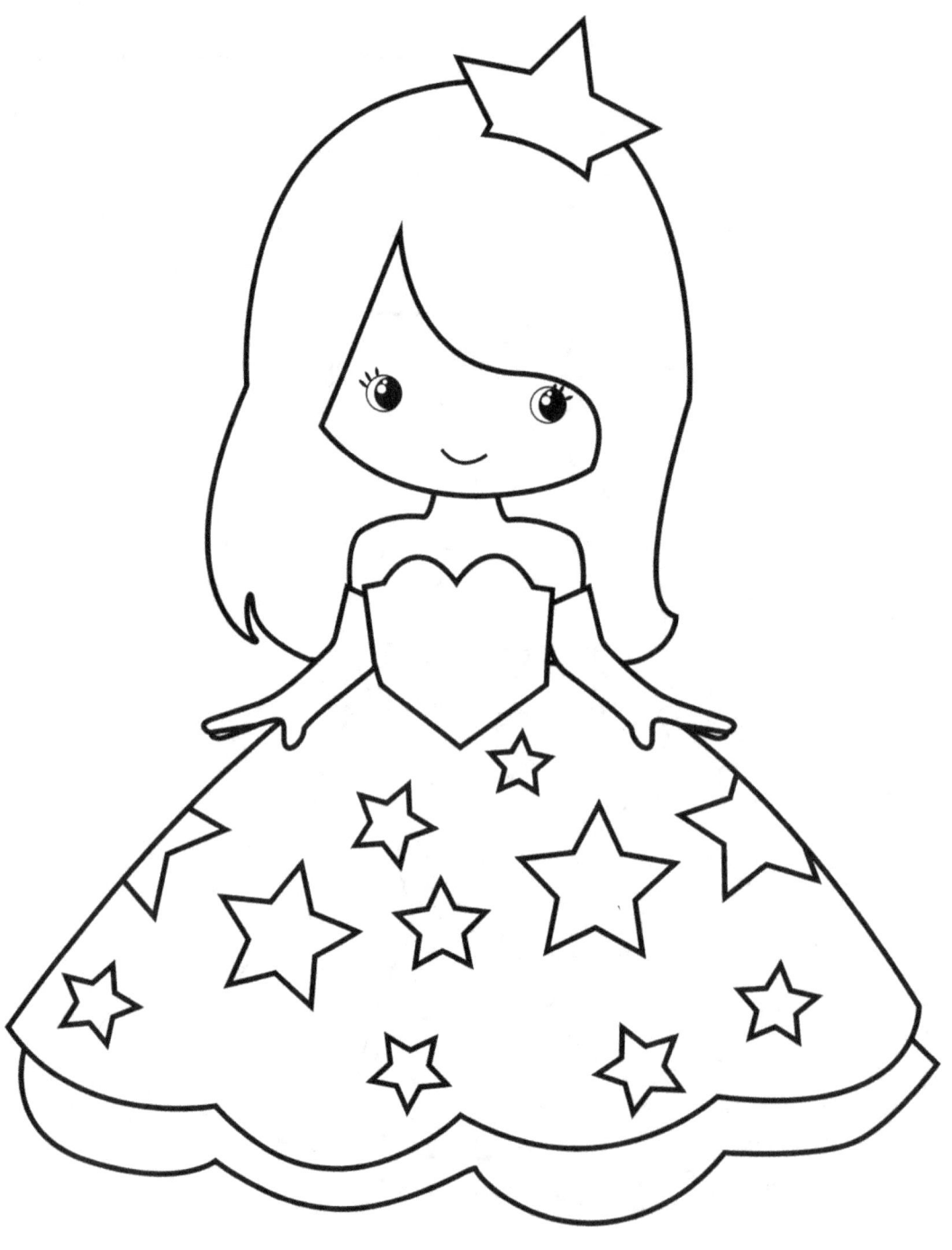

NAME: _____

KING

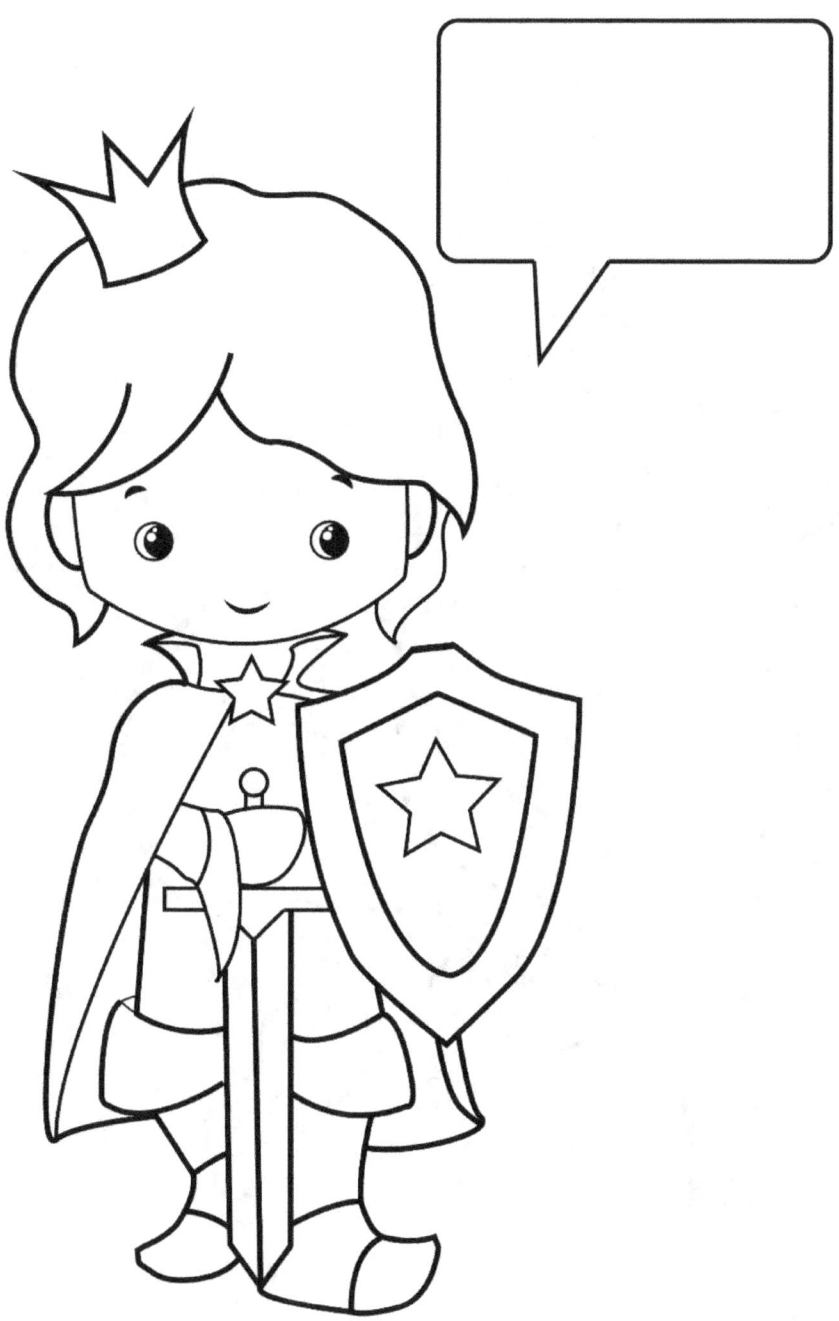

NAME:

UNICORN

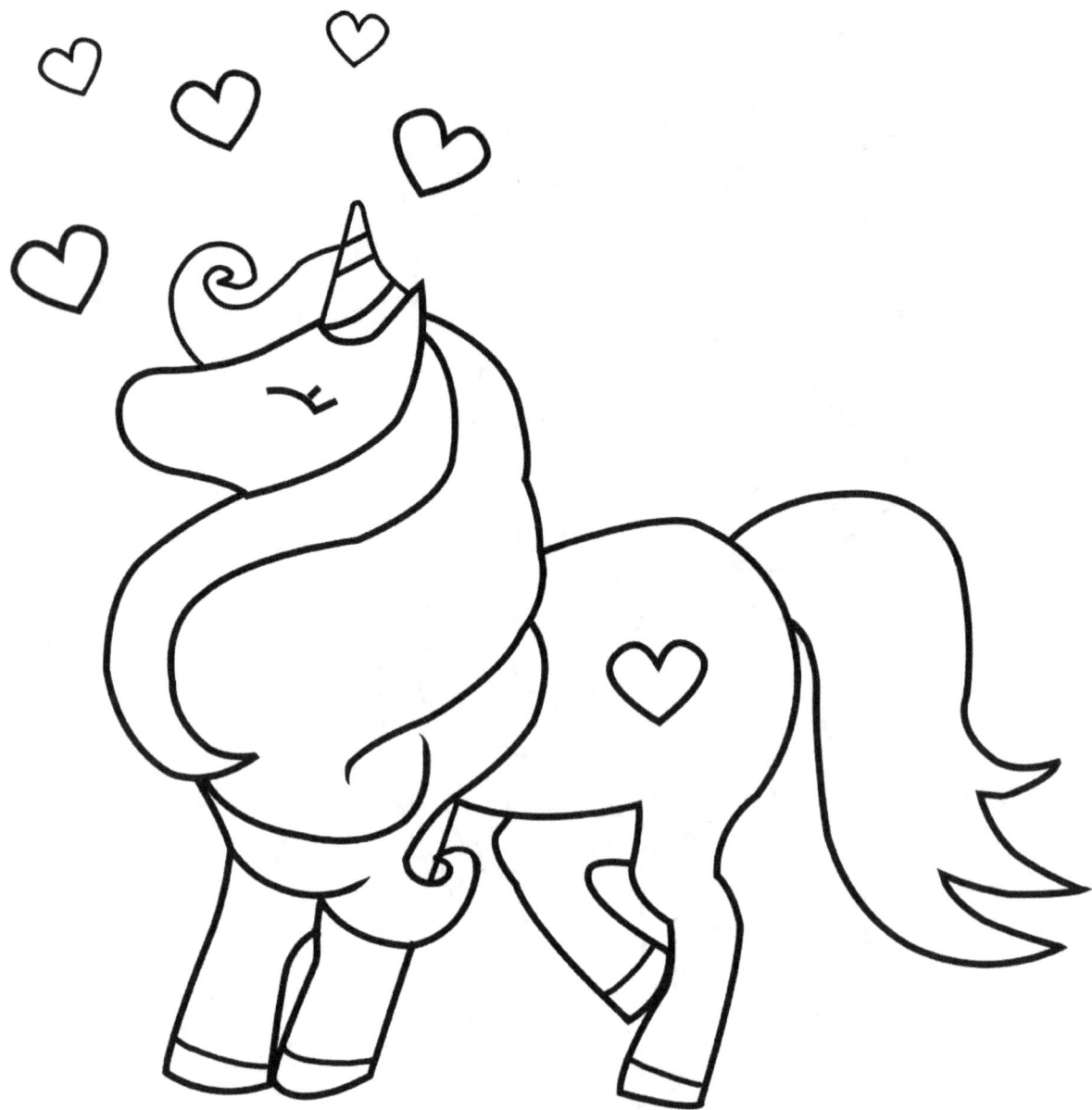

NAME:

CARRIAGE

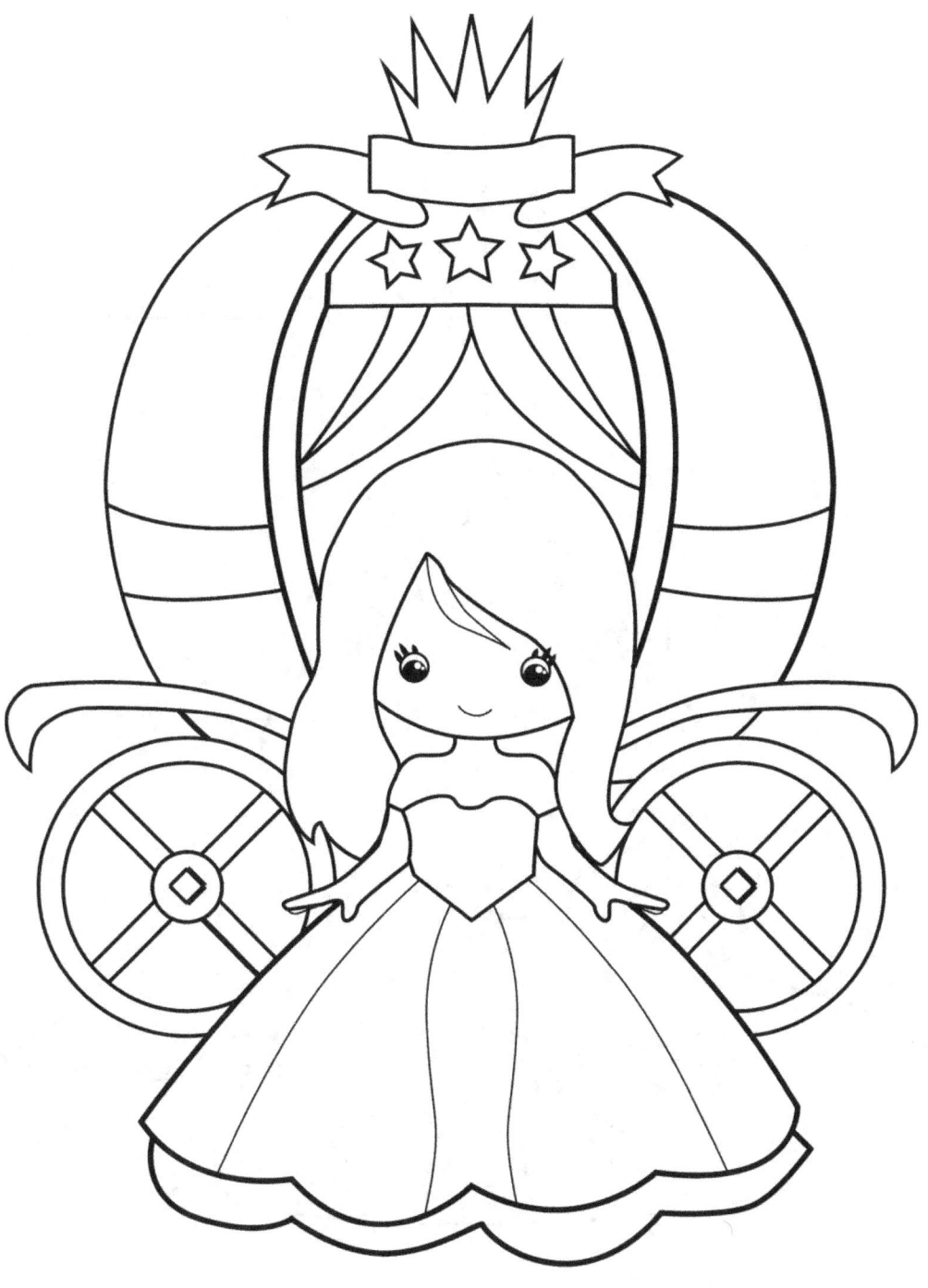

NAME:

FROG

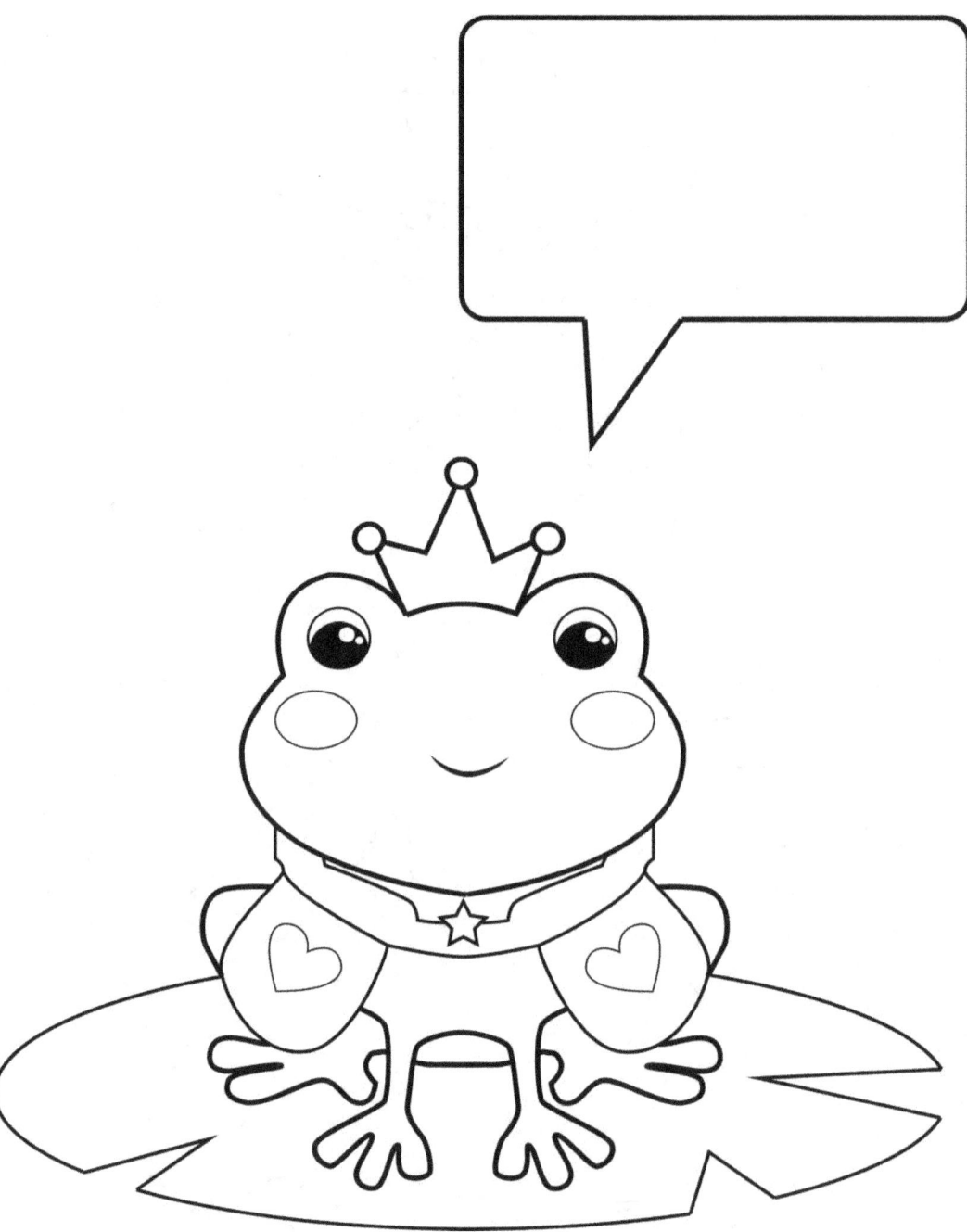

NAME:

PRINCESS

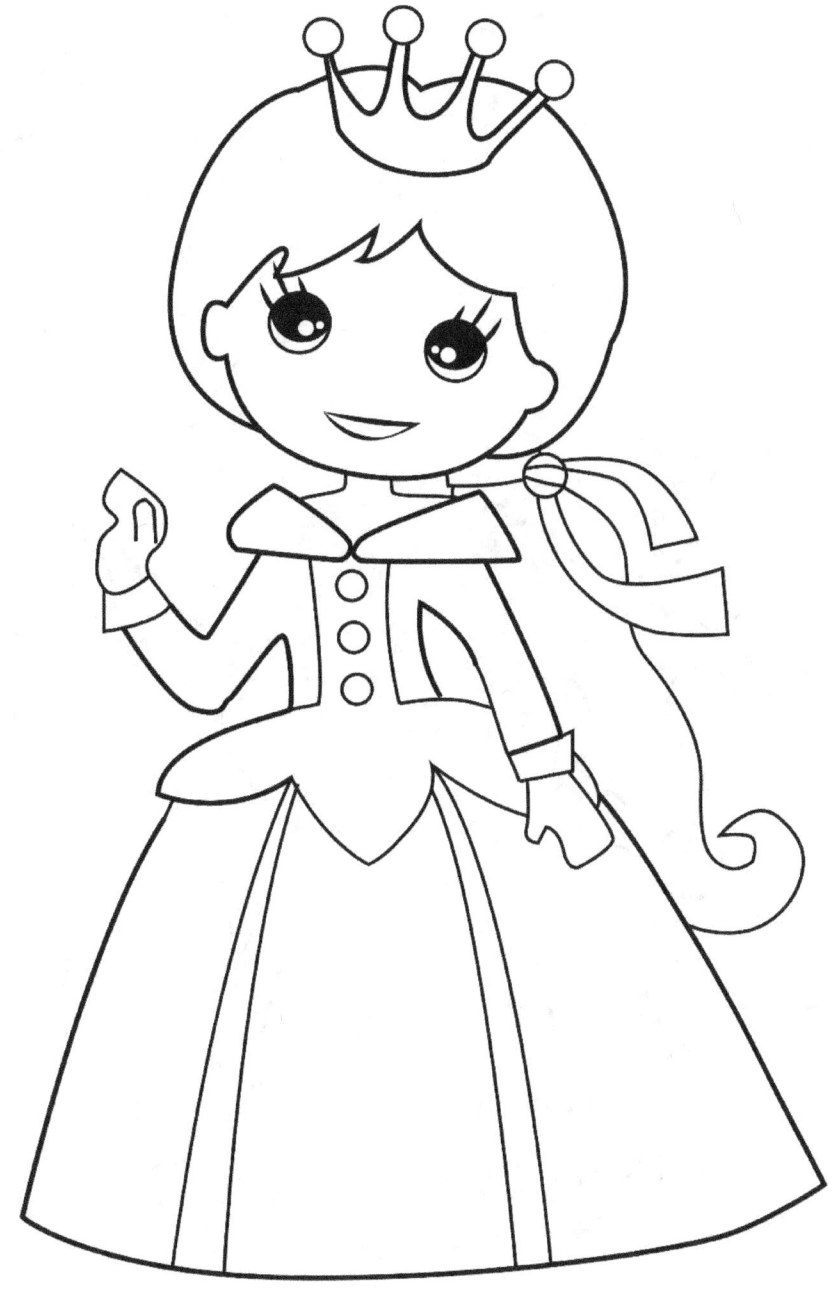

NAME:

QUEEN

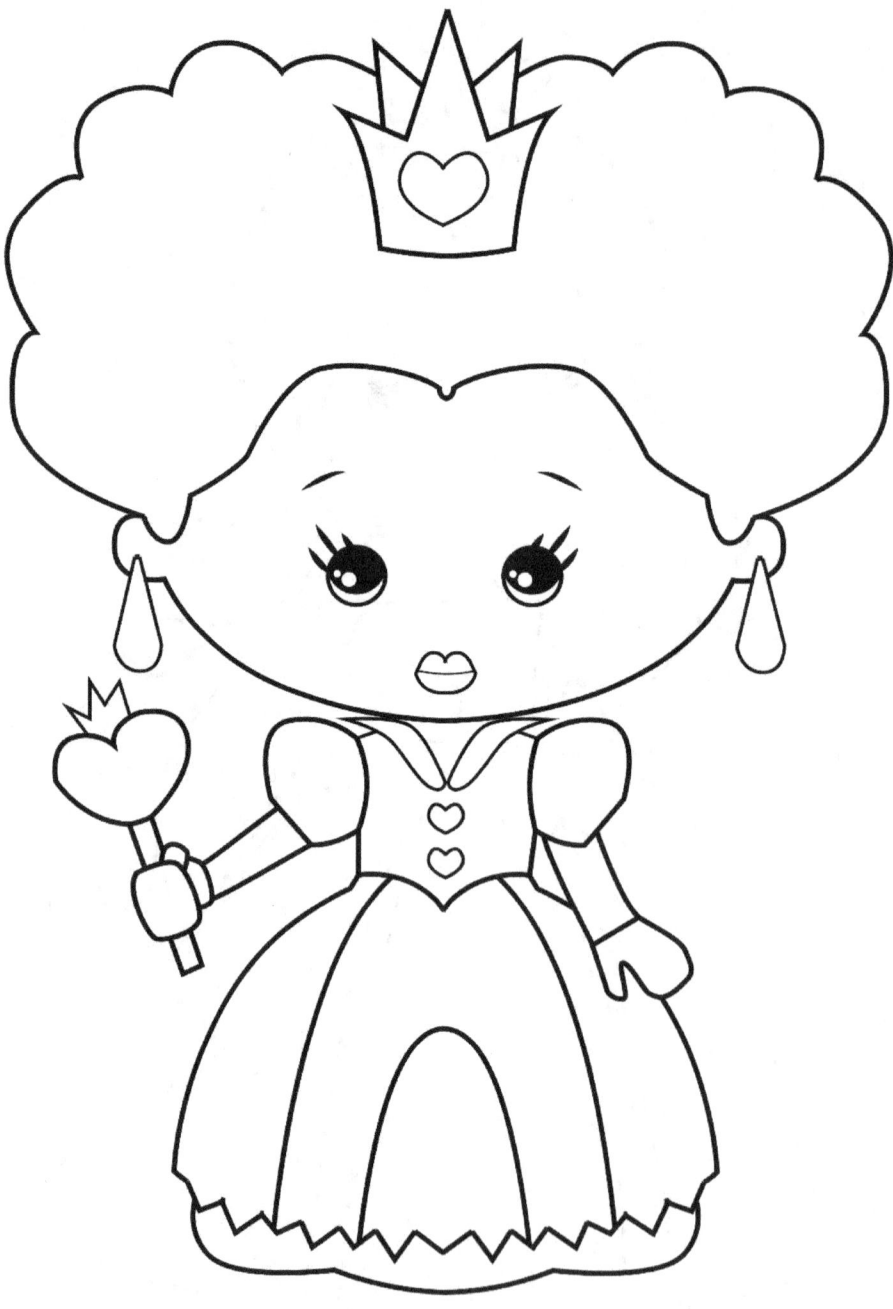

NAME:

KNIGHT JUNIOR

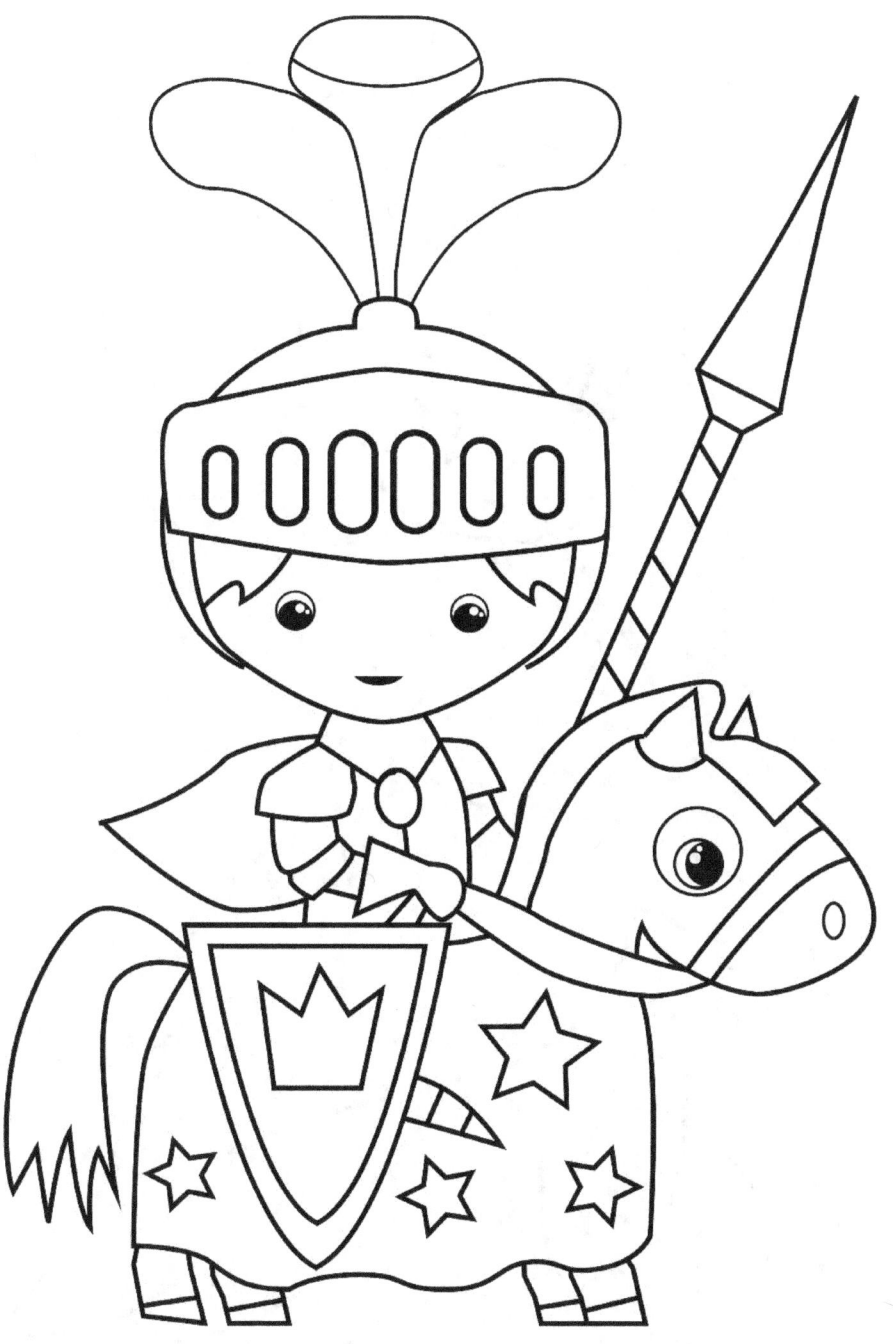

NAME:

PRINCESS

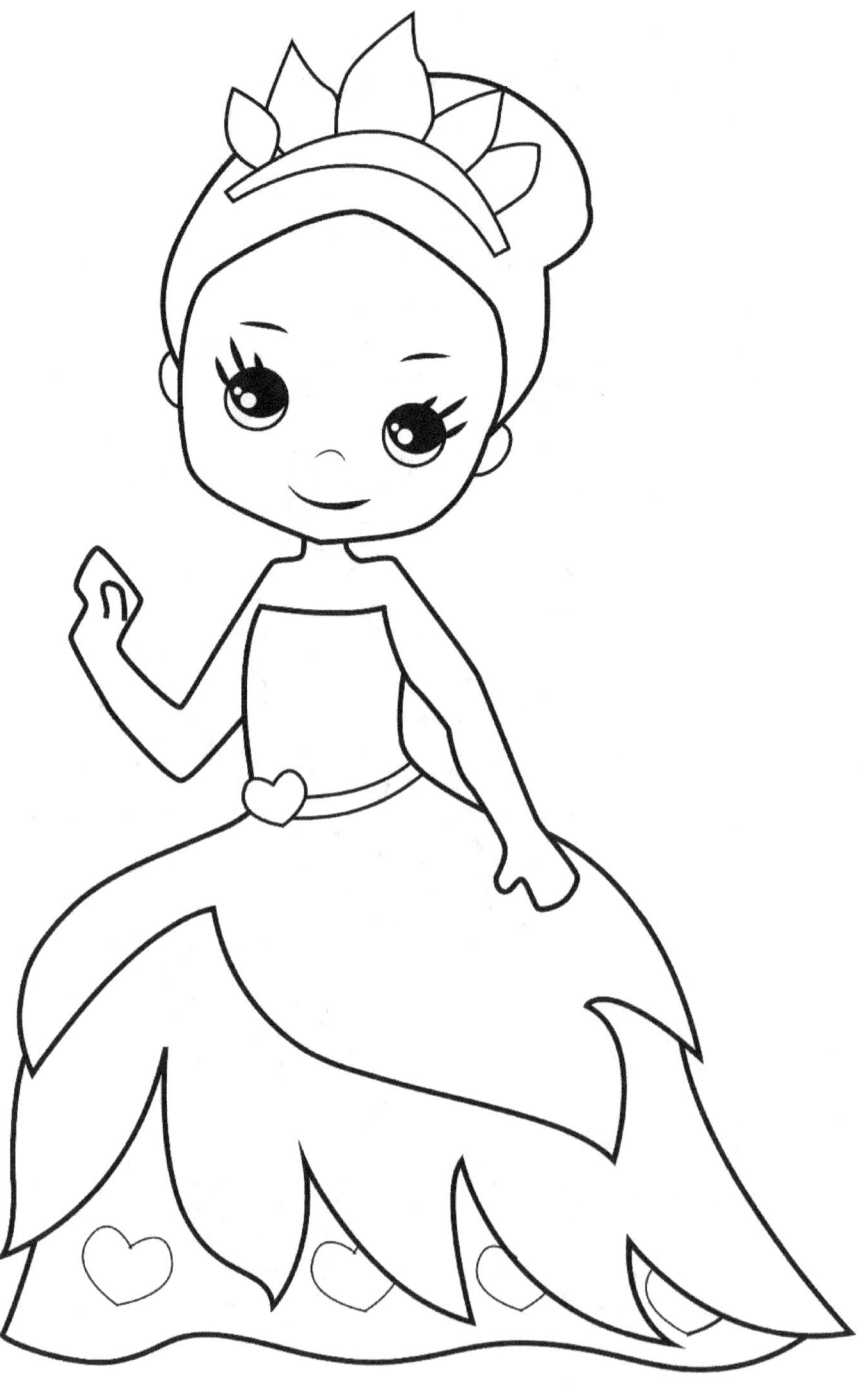

NAME:

GUARD

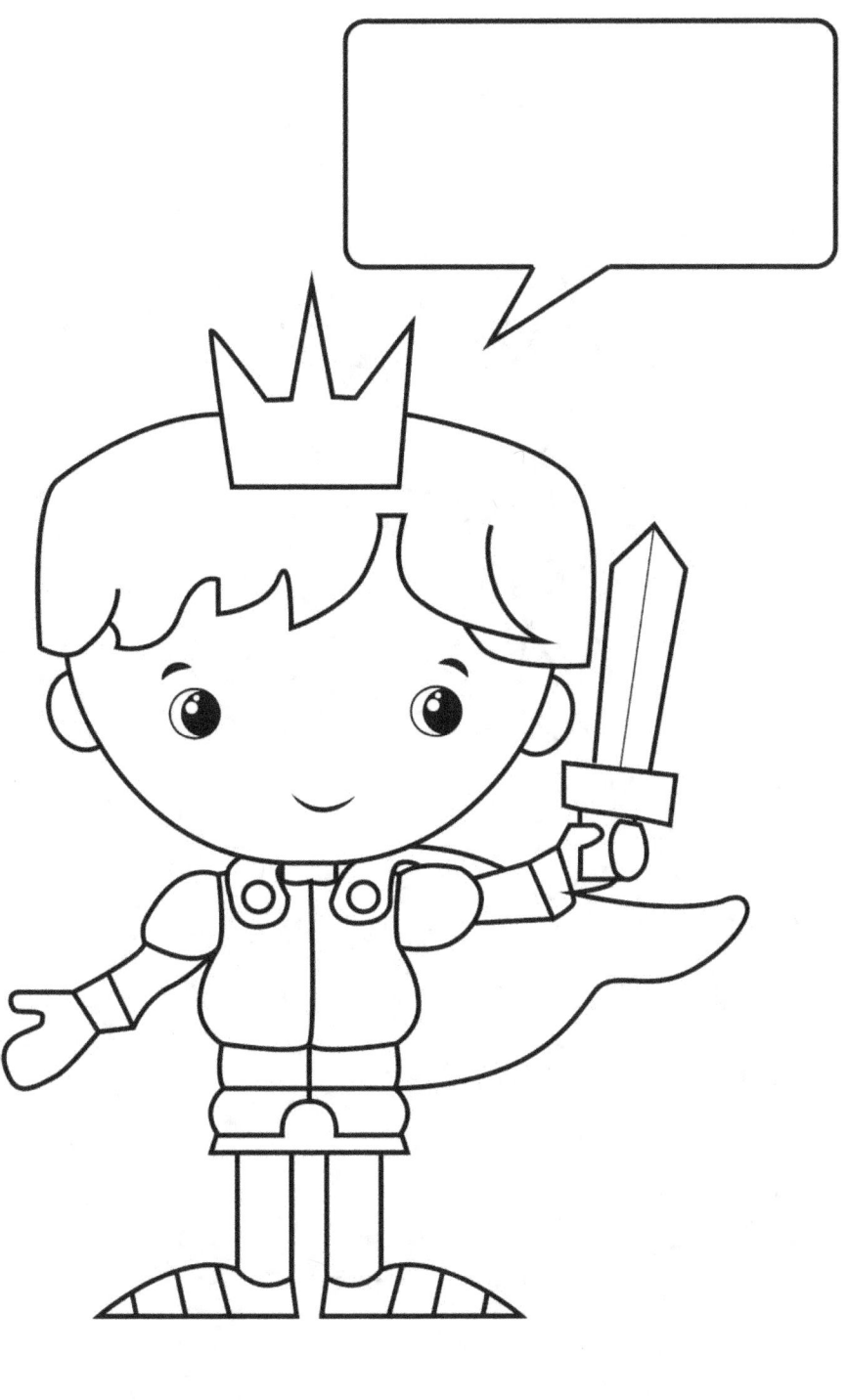

NAME:

PRINCESS

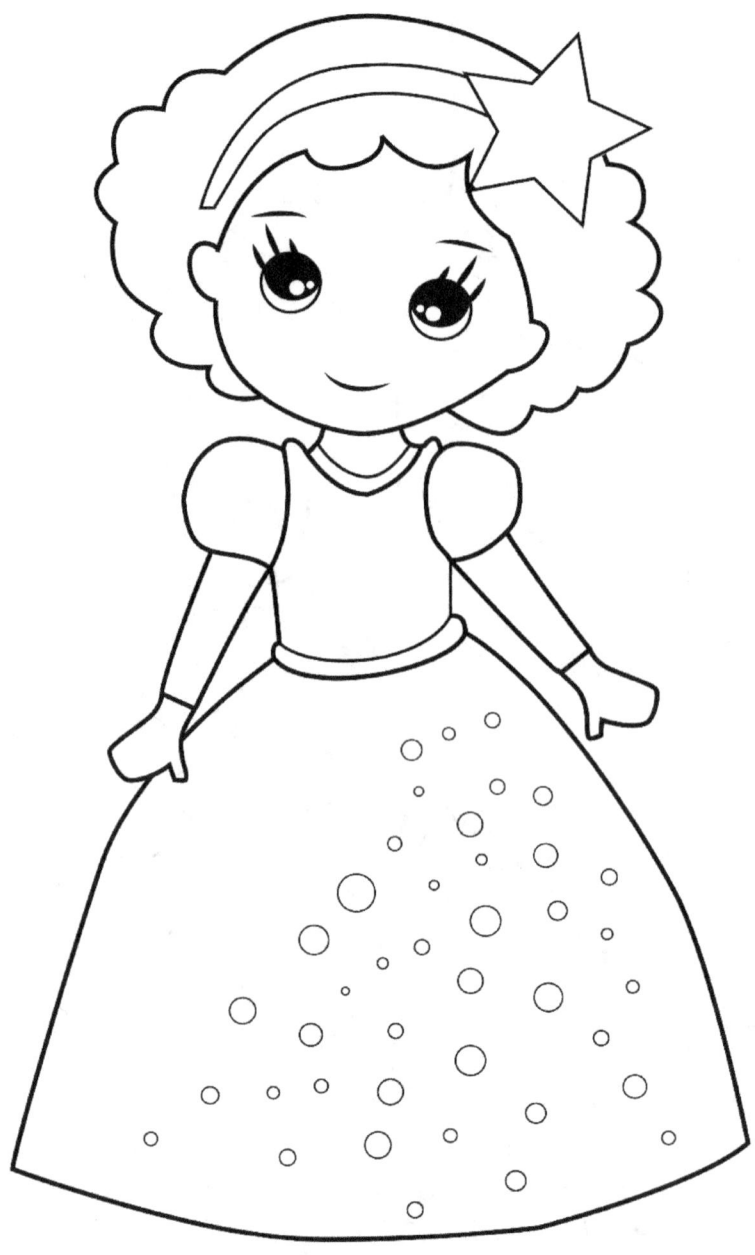

NAME: _____

PRINCESS

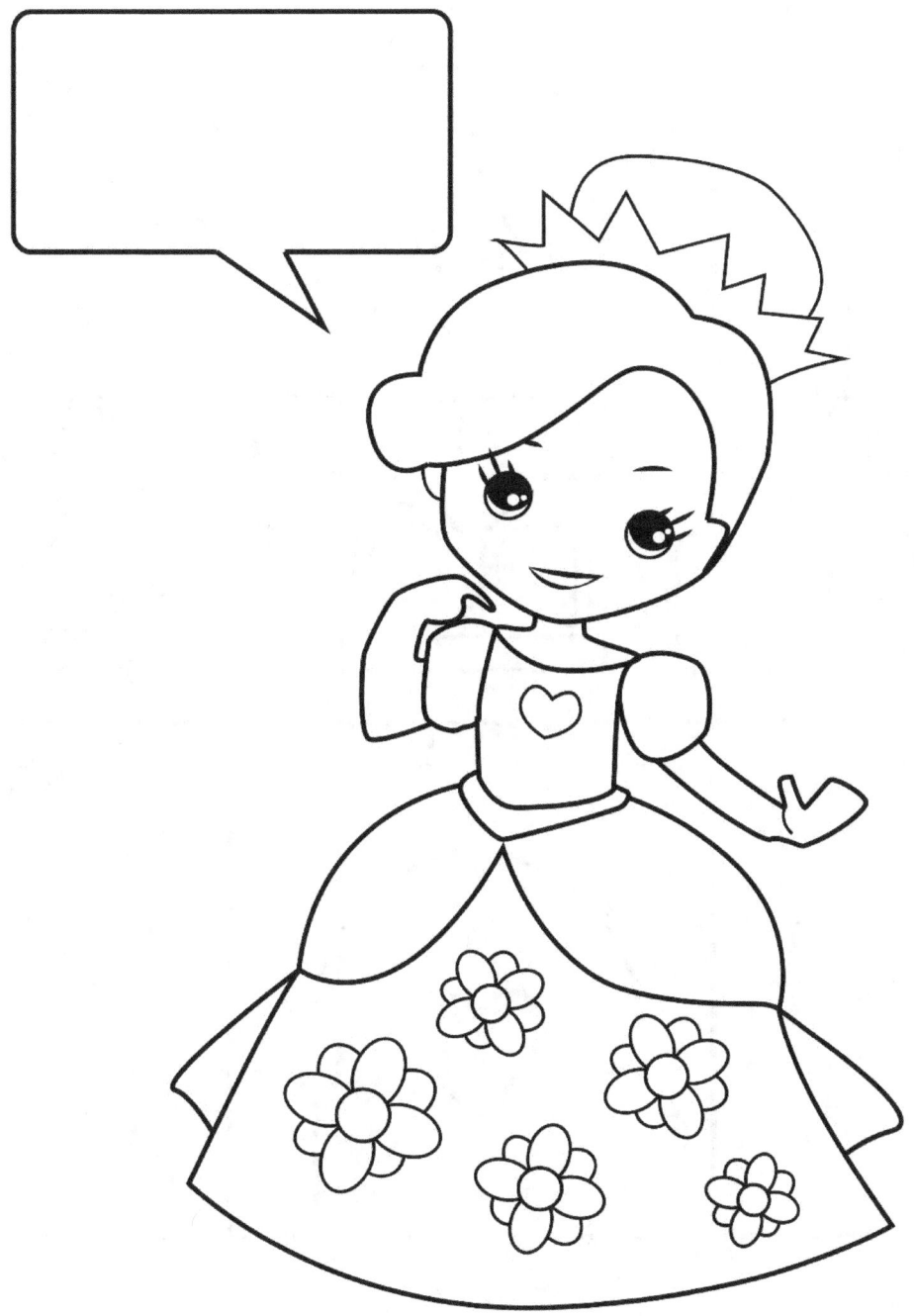

NAME:

CASTLE

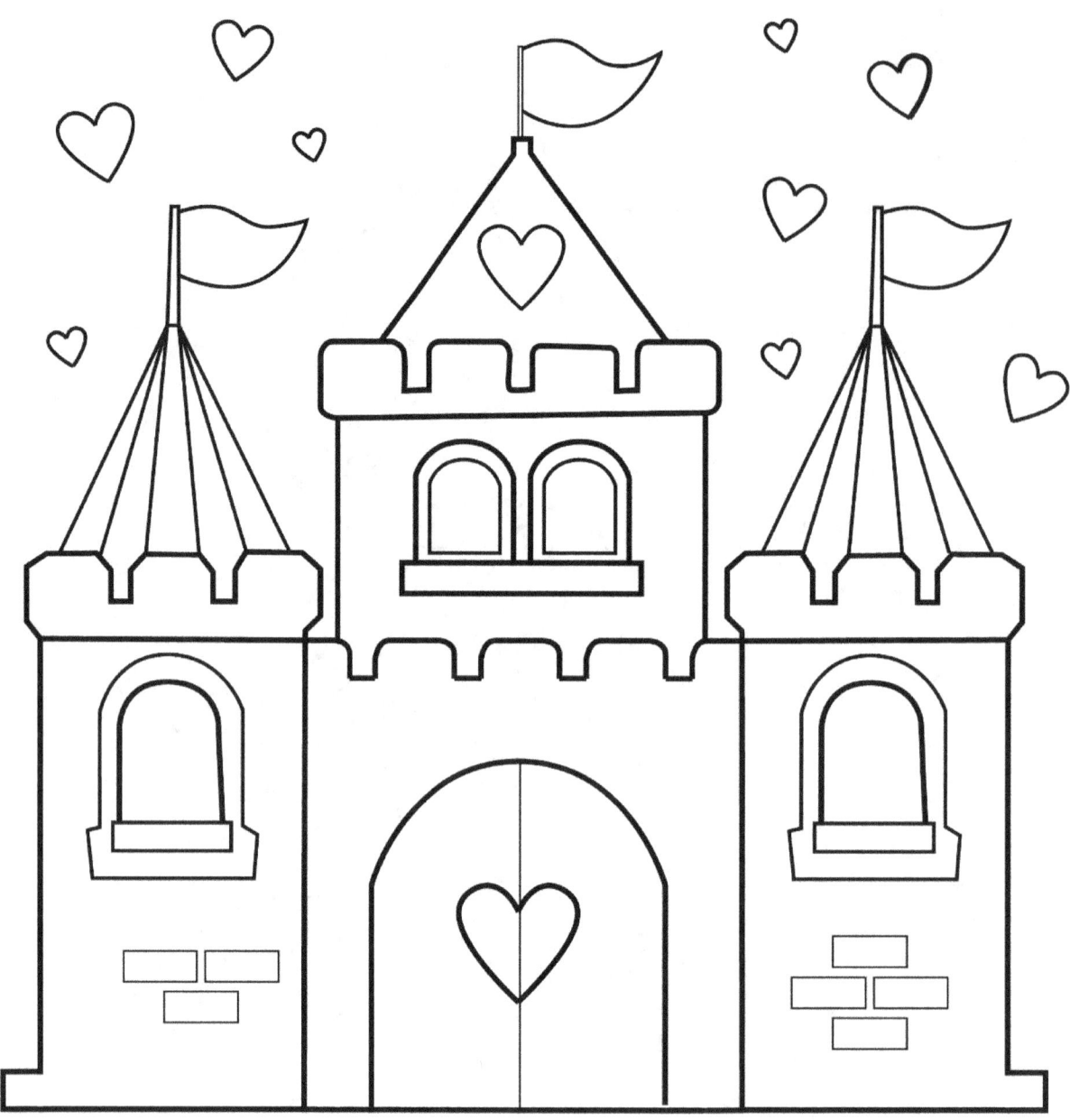

NAME:

PRINCESS

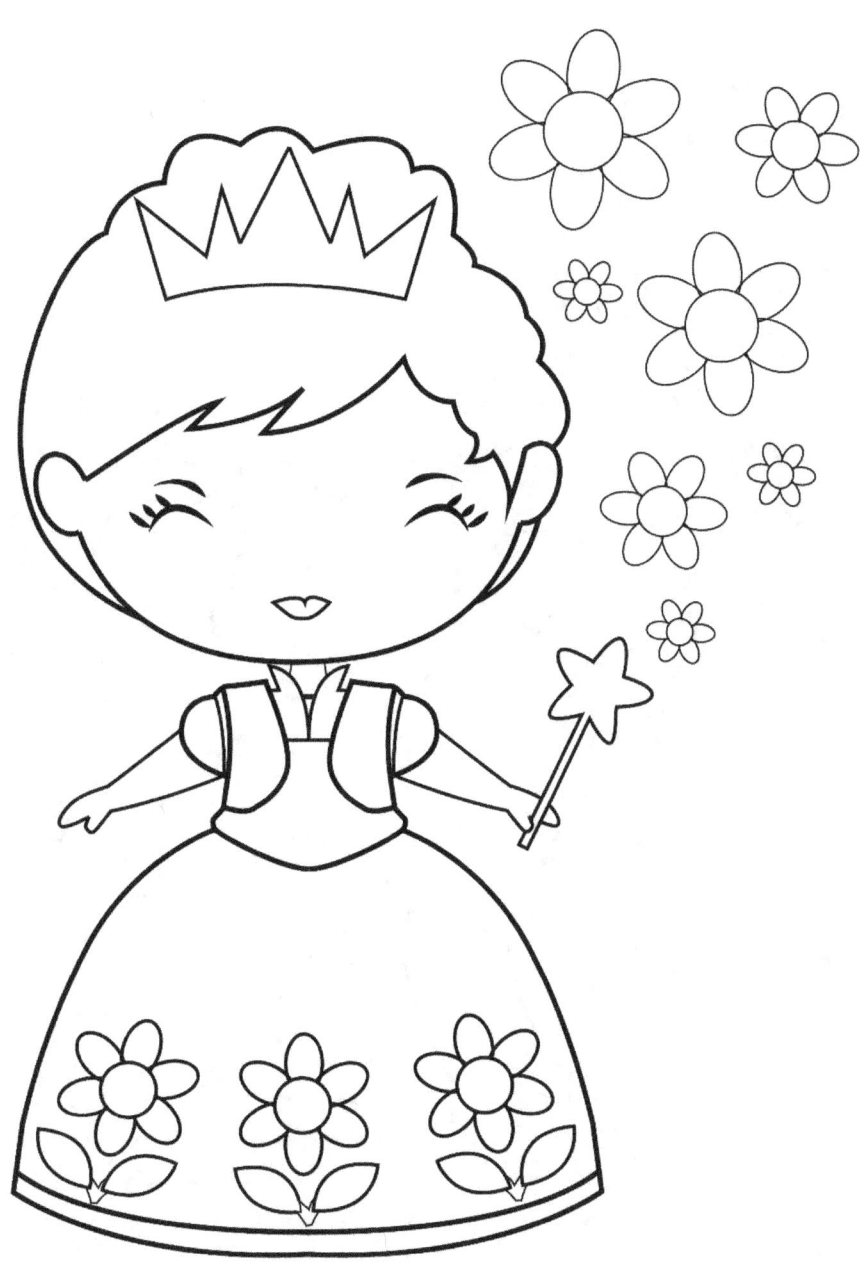

NAME:

HORSE

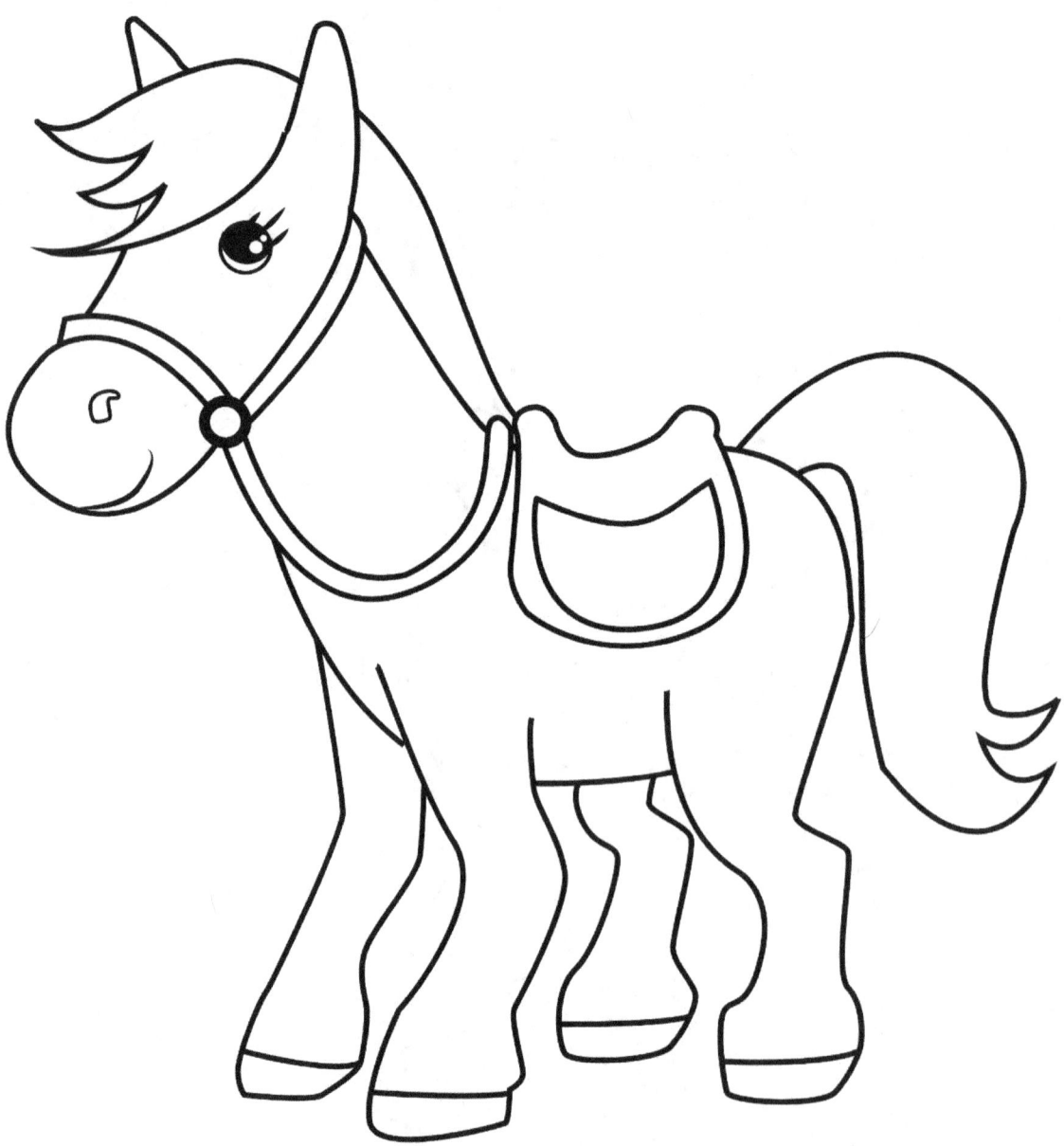

NAME:

FAIRY

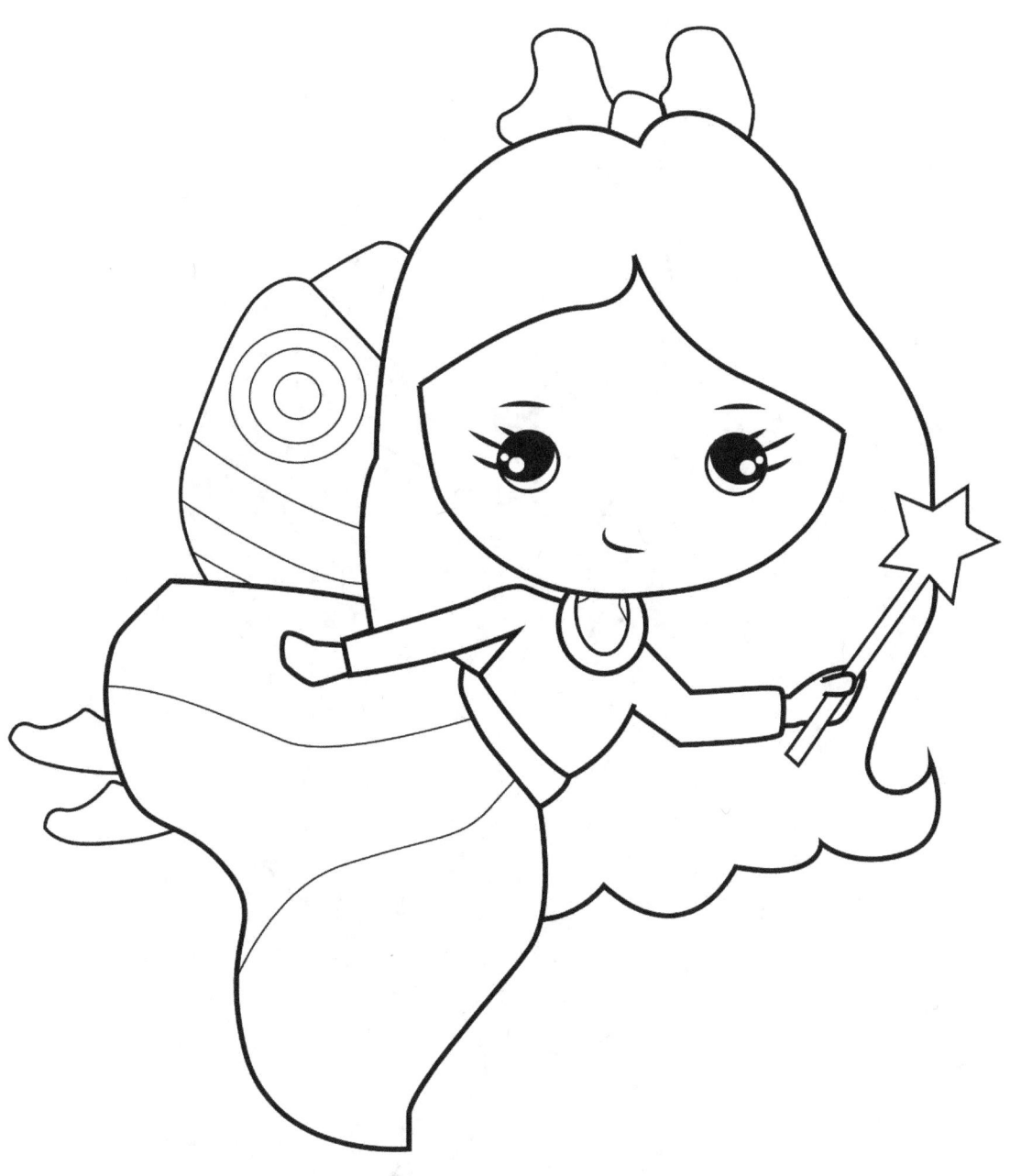

NAME:

MERMAID

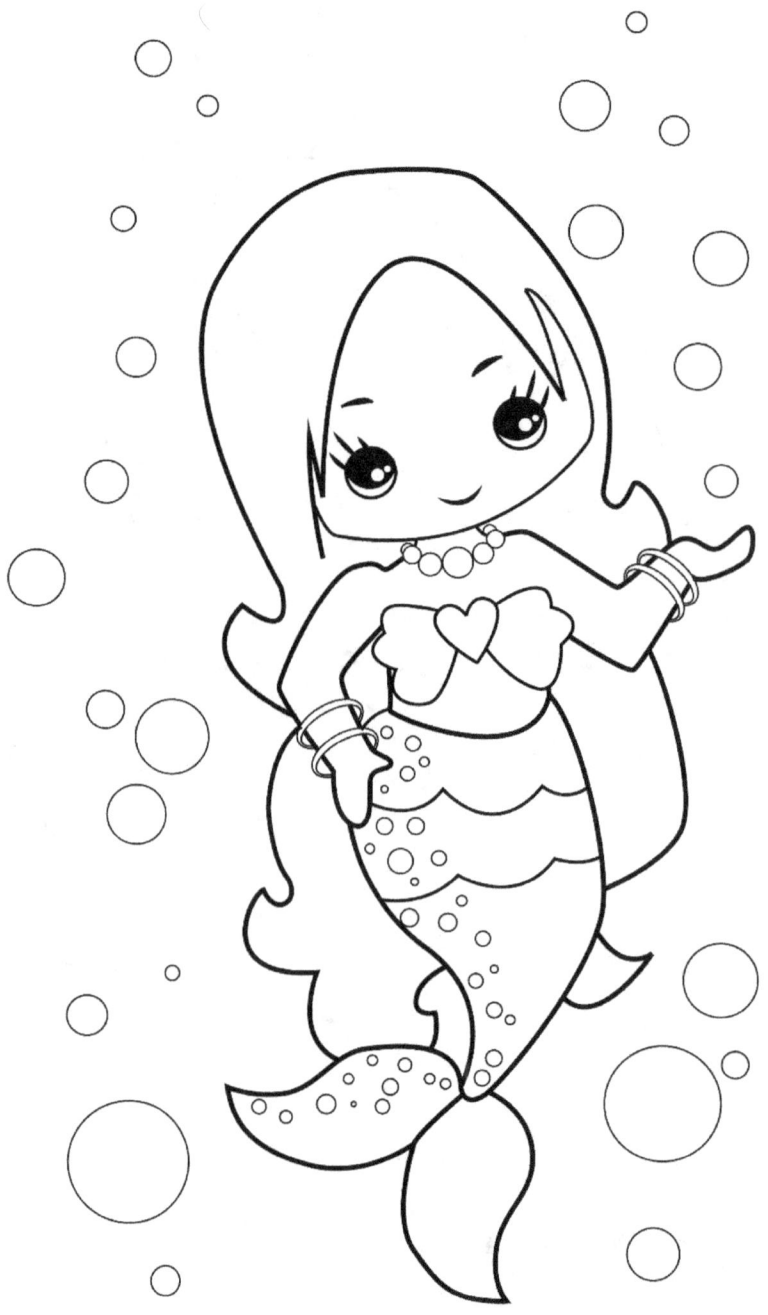

NAME:

BIRDS

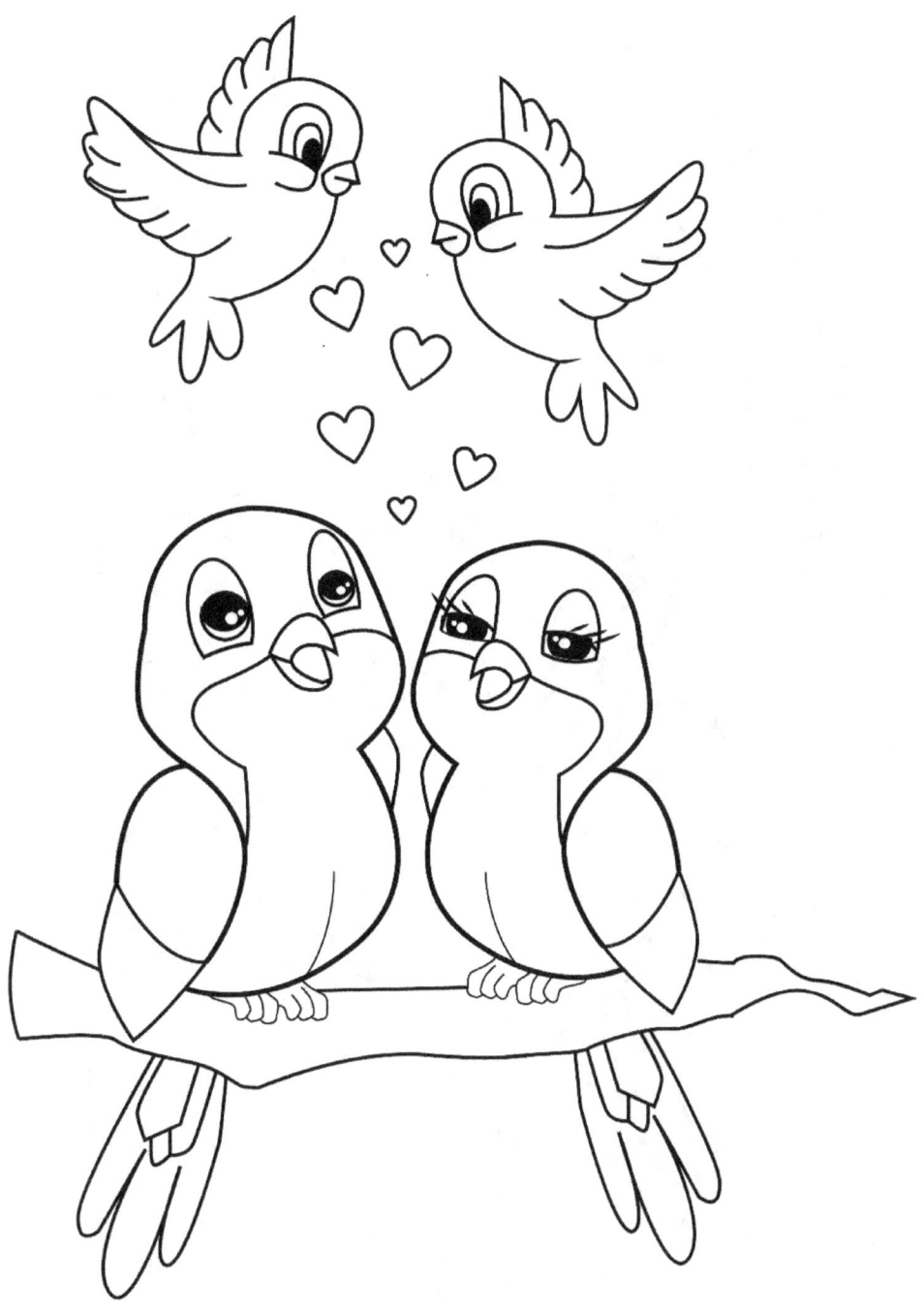

NAME:

PRINCESS

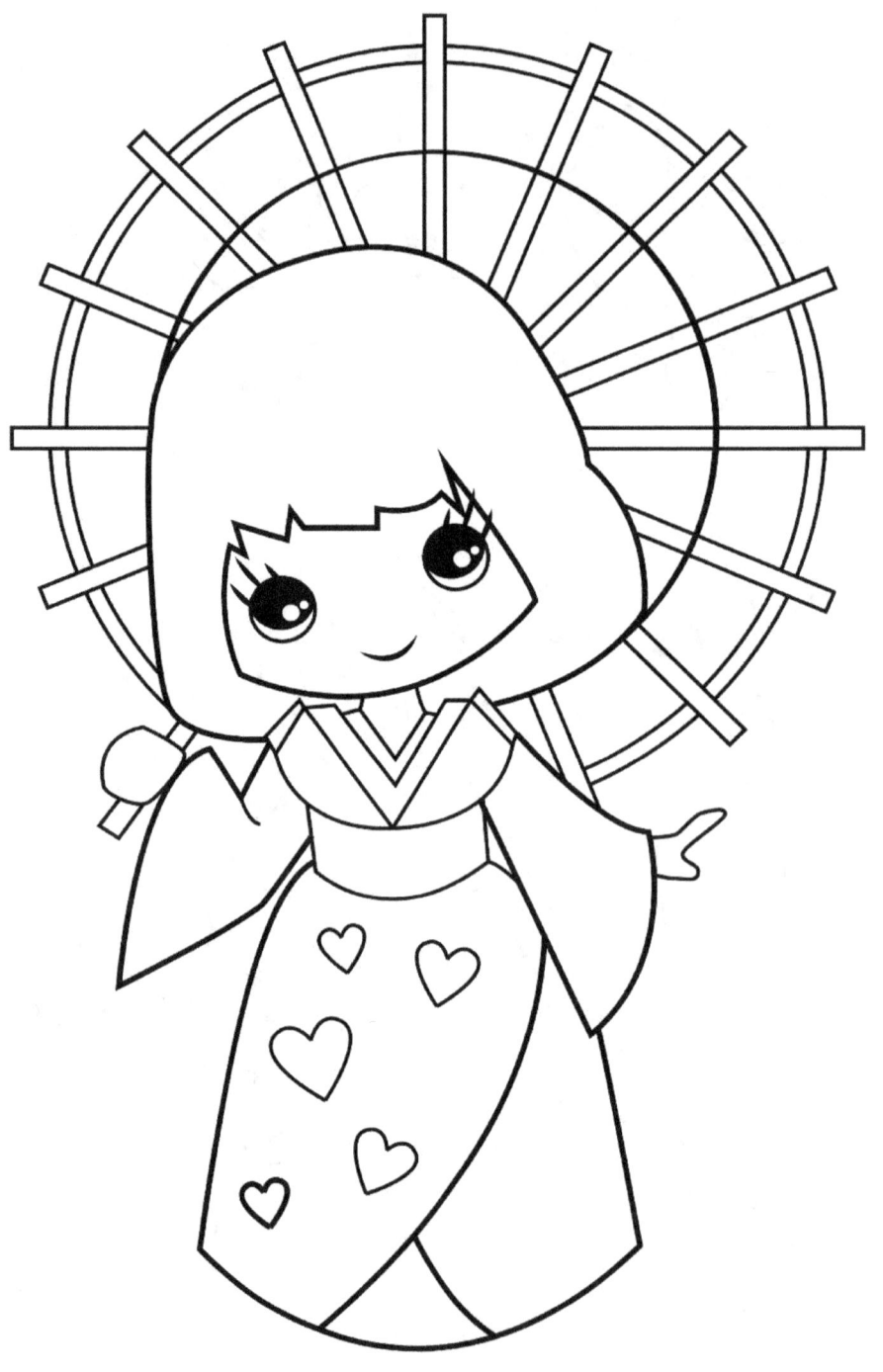

NAME:

WITCHER

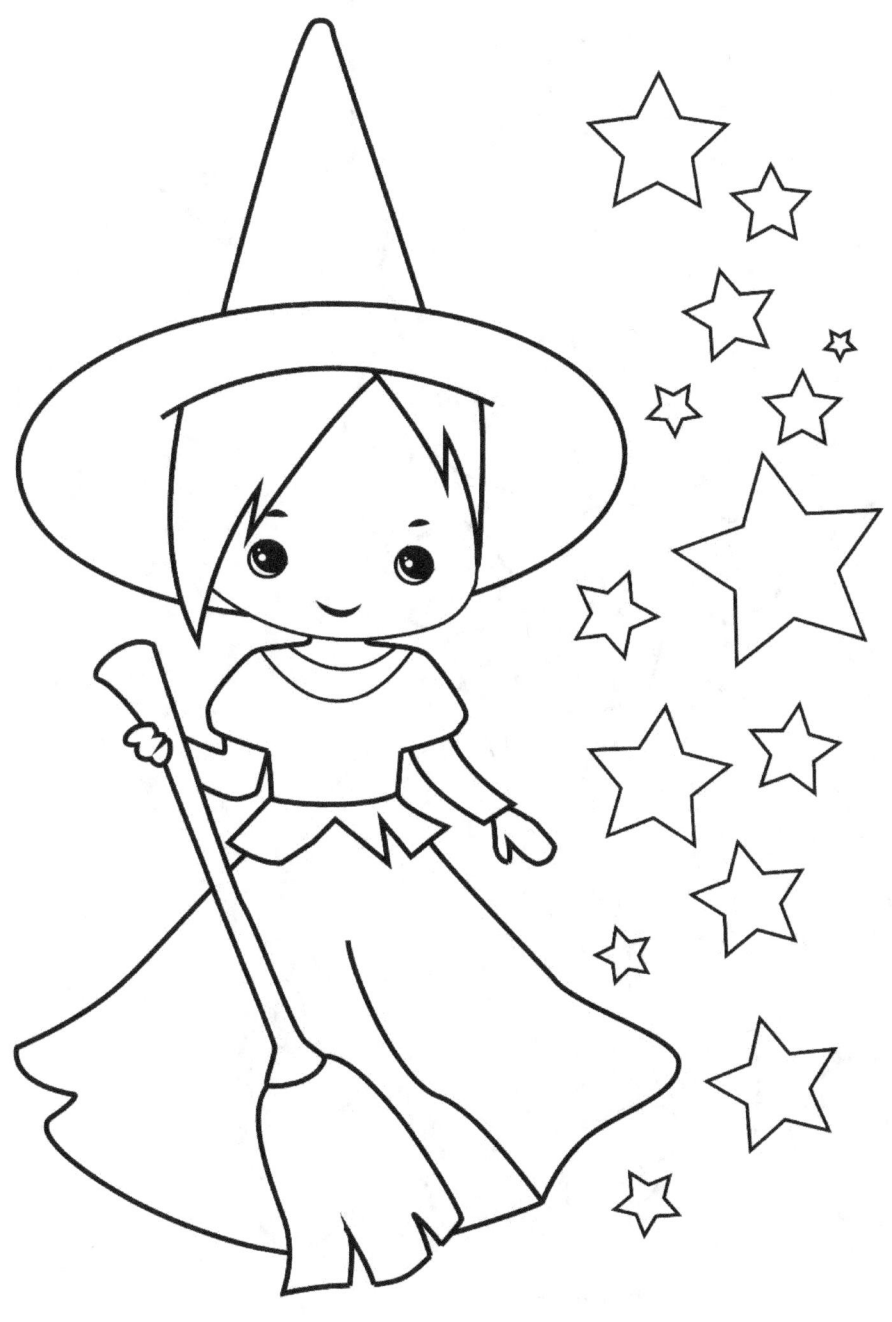

NAME:

PRINCESS

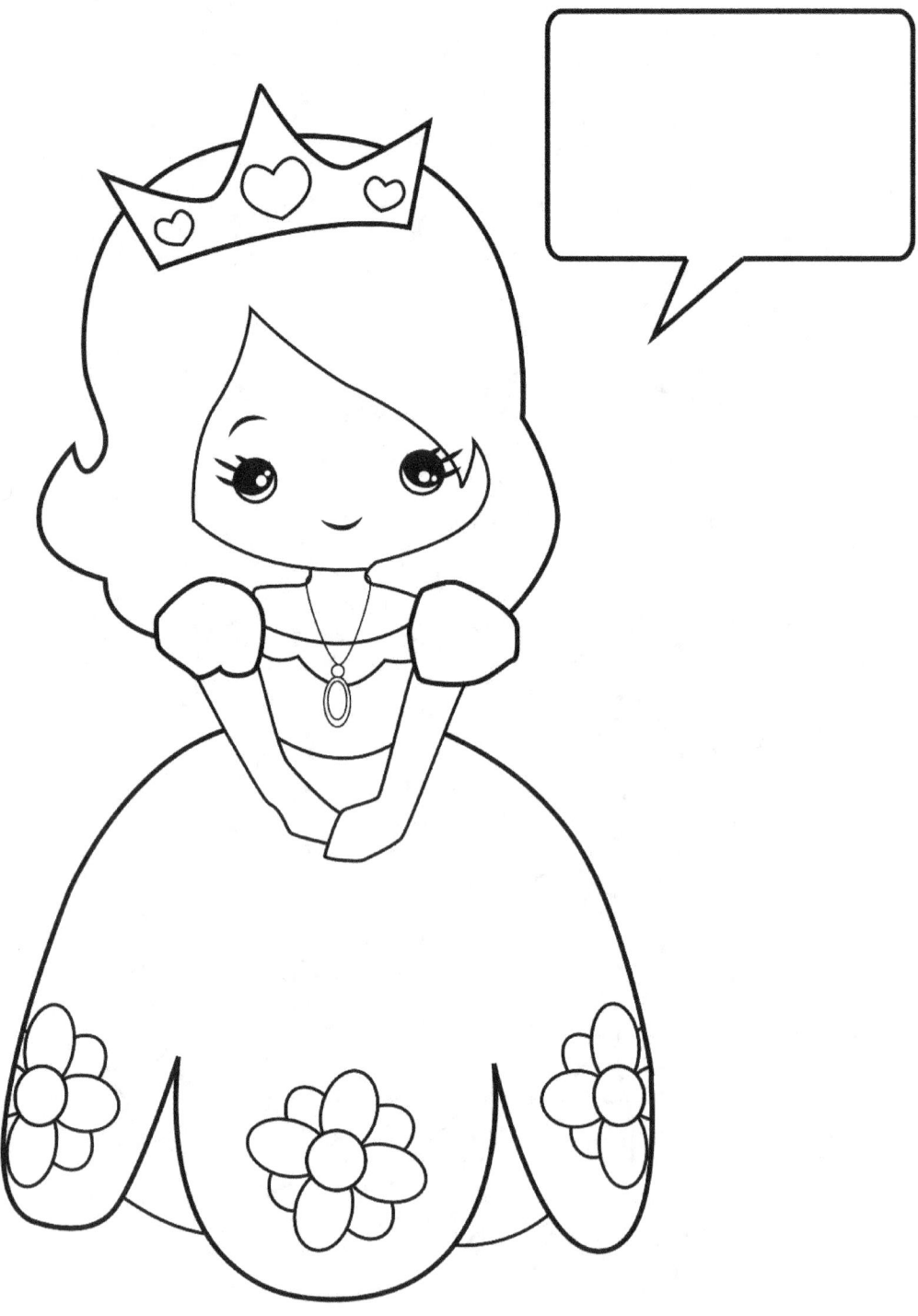

NAME:

PRINCESS

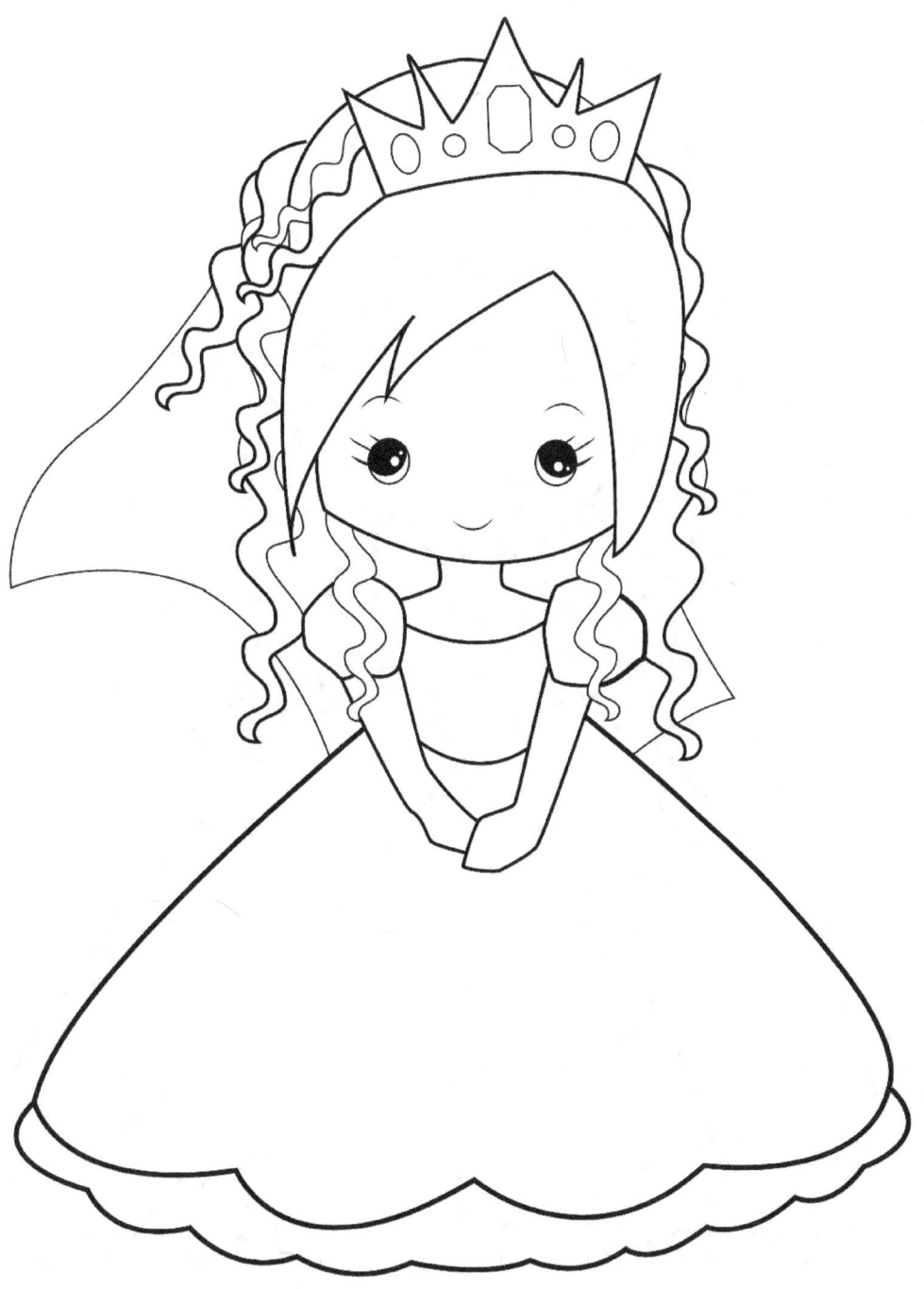

NAME:

QUEEN

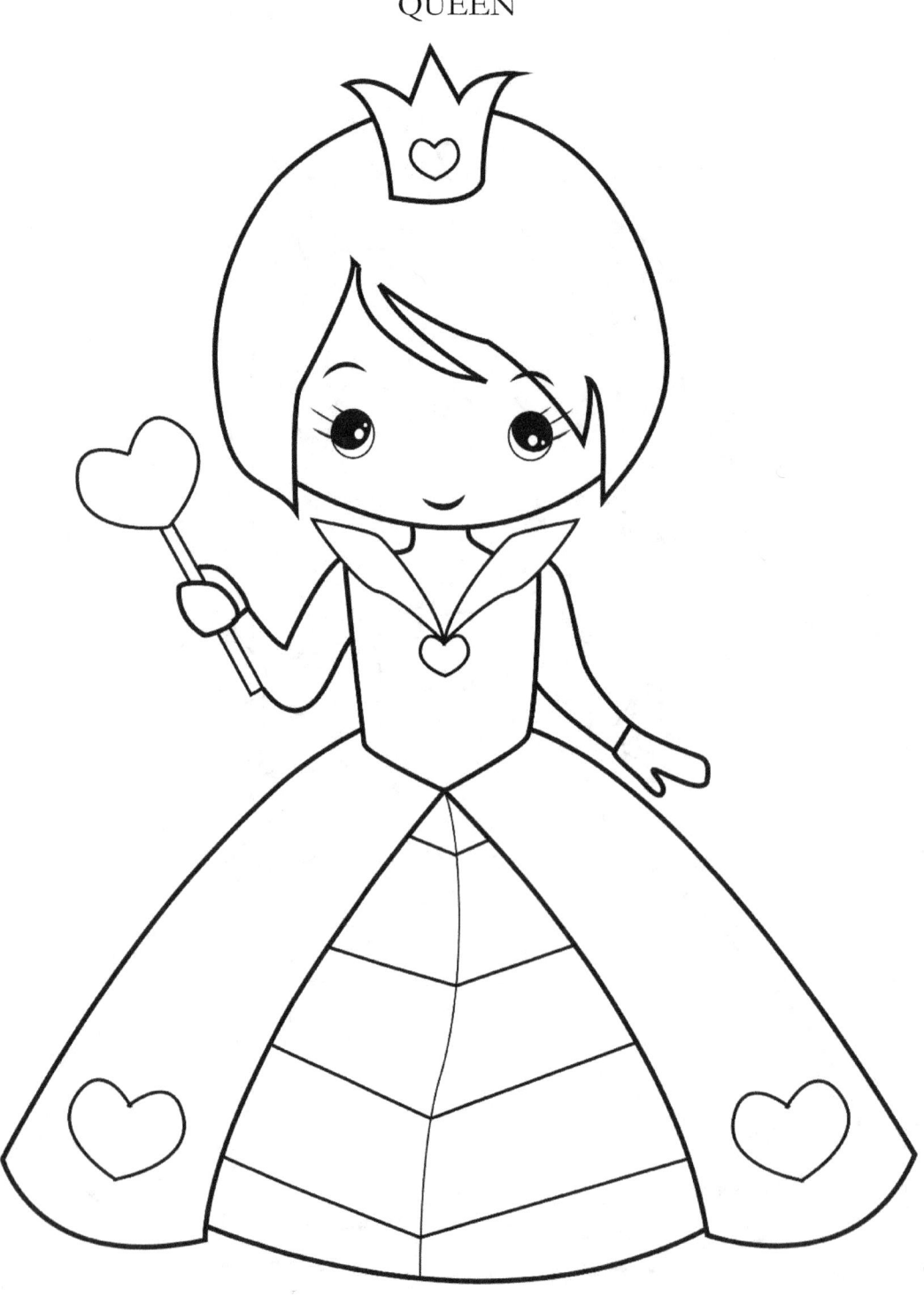

NAME:

FAIRY

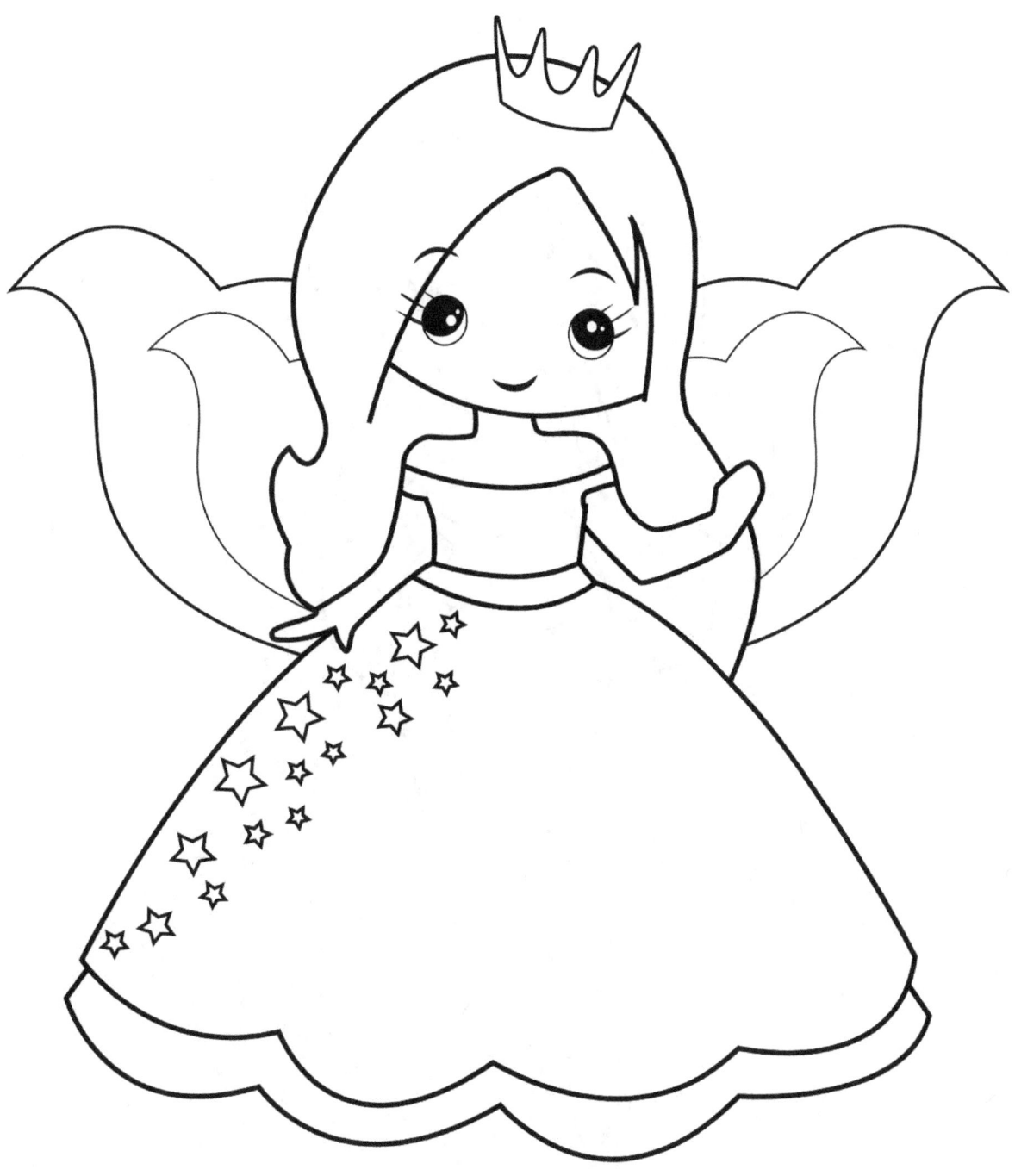

NAME:

MERMAID

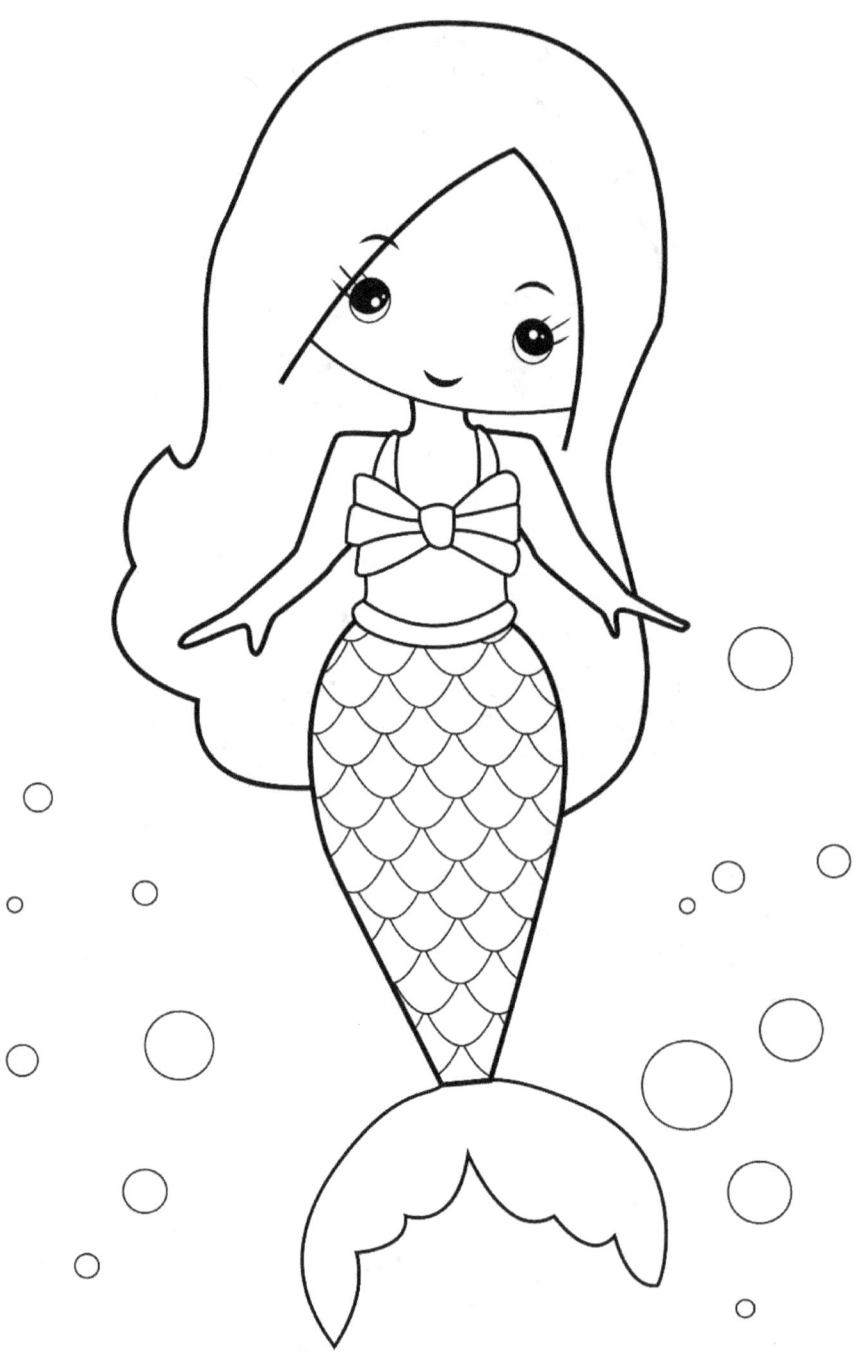

NAME:

QUEEN

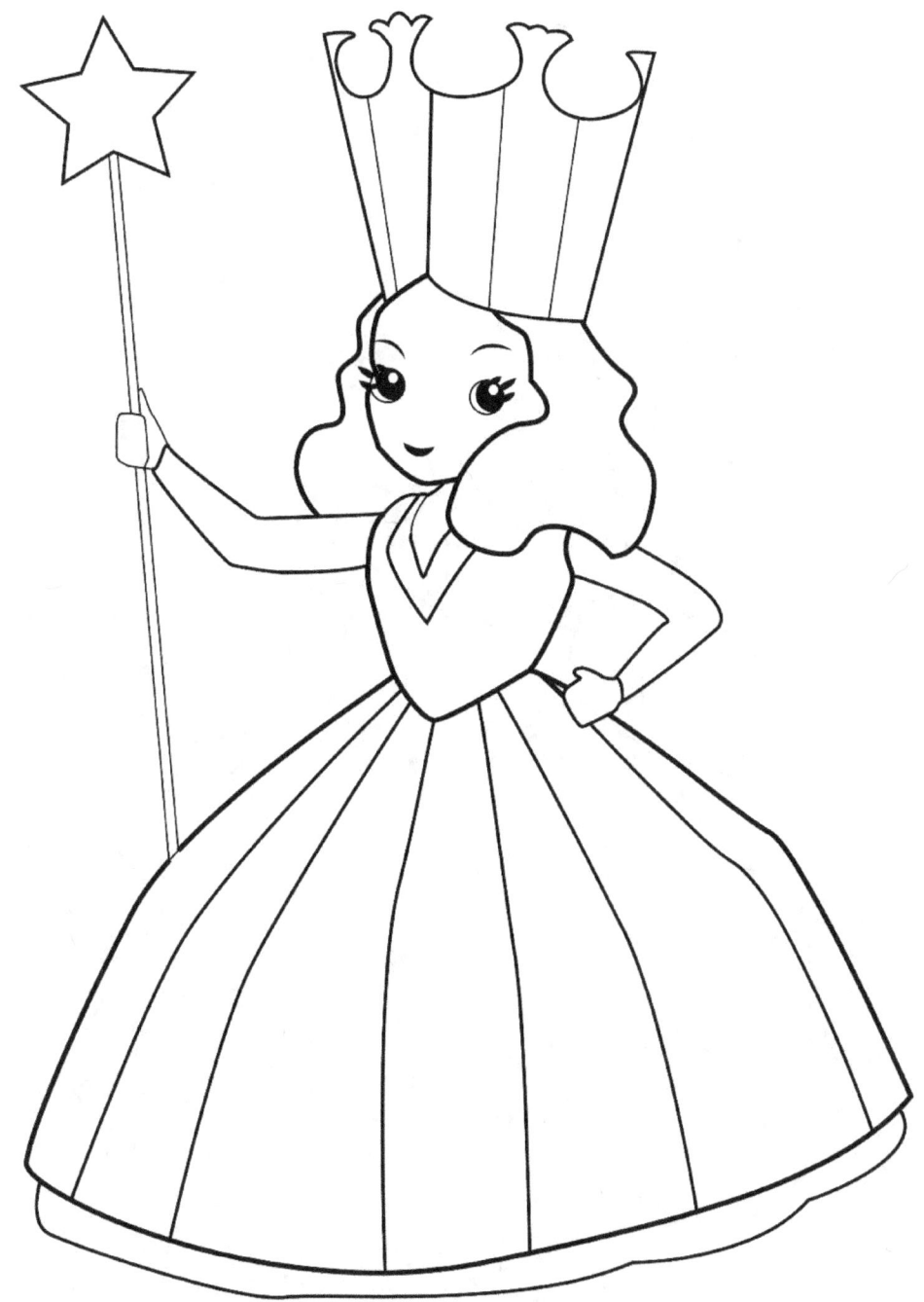

NAME:

PRINCESS

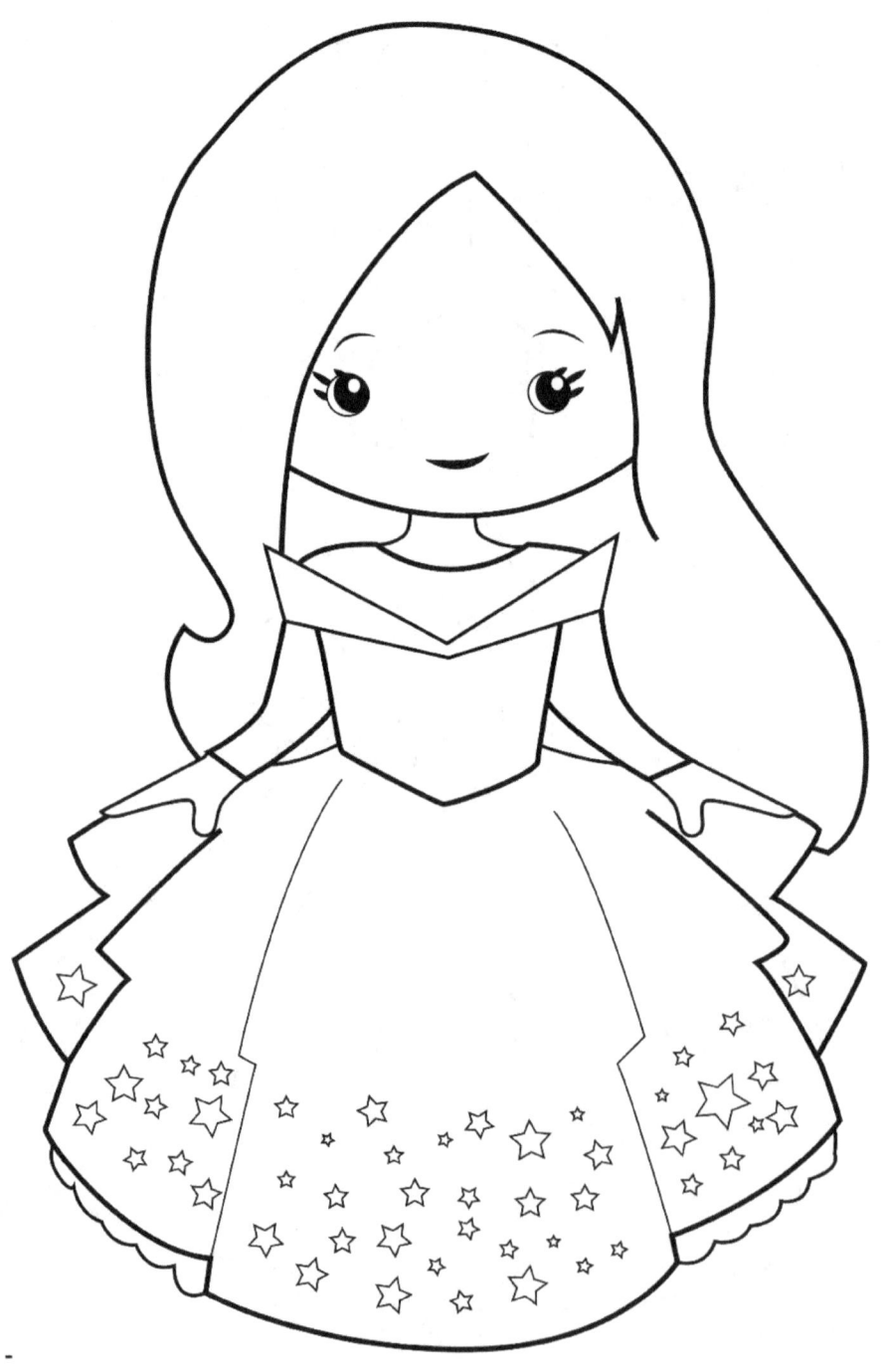

NAME:

PRINCESS

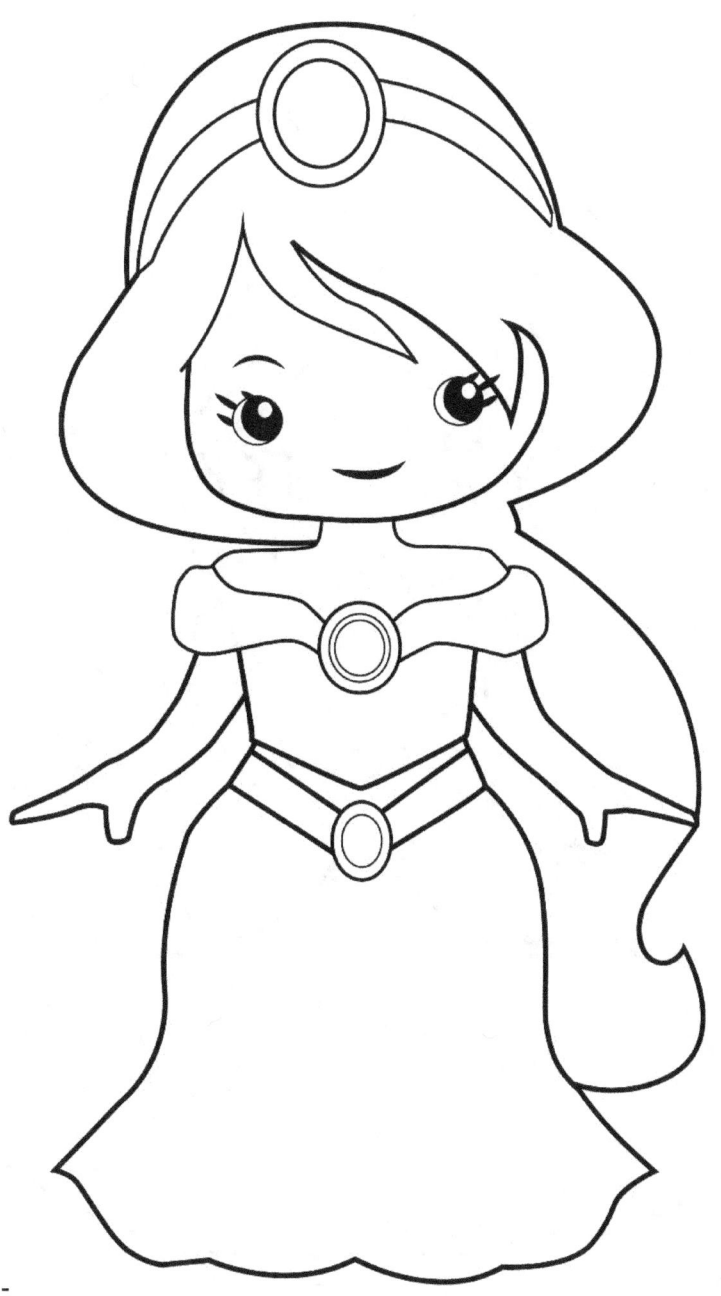

NAME:

PRINCESS

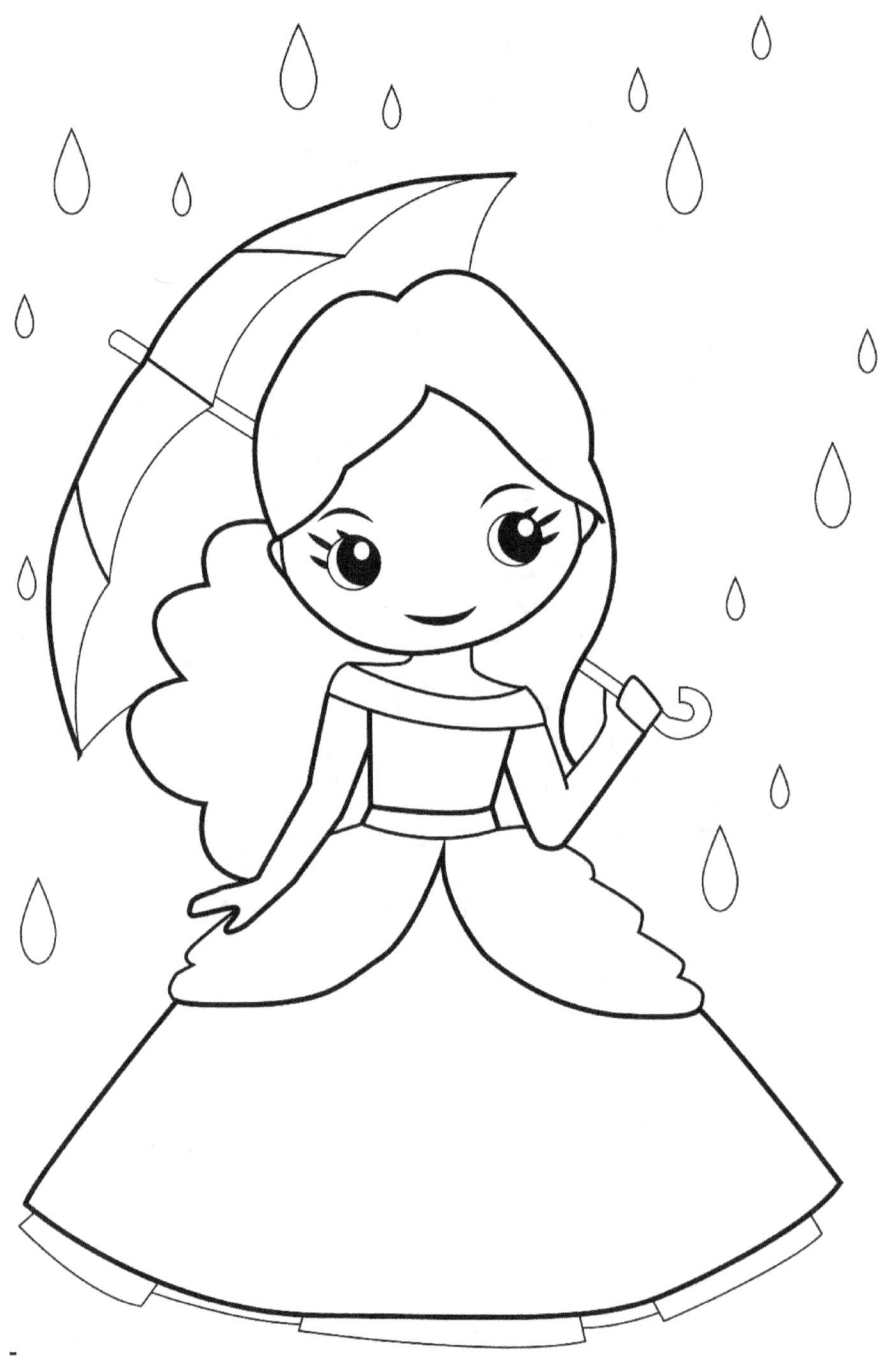

NAME:

FAIRY

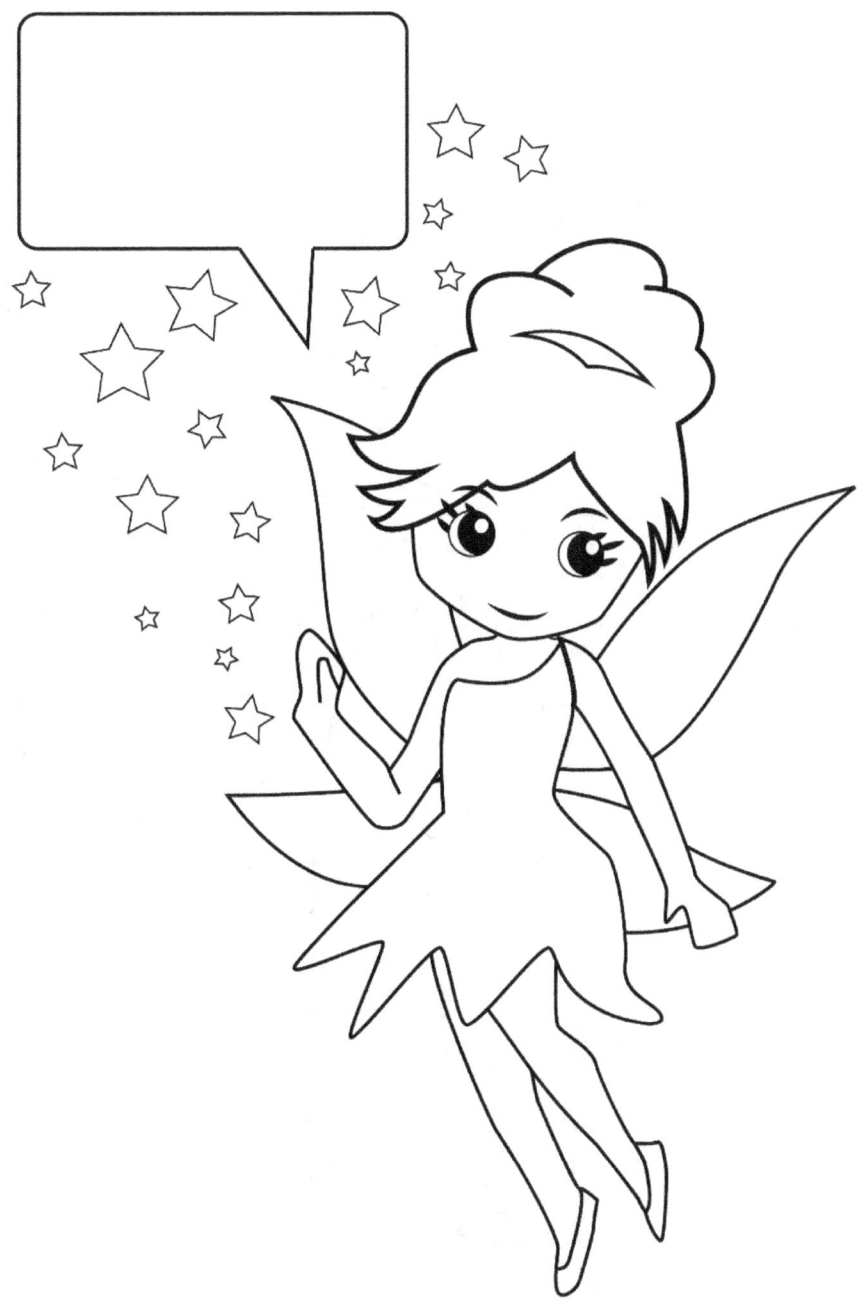

NAME:

PRINCESS

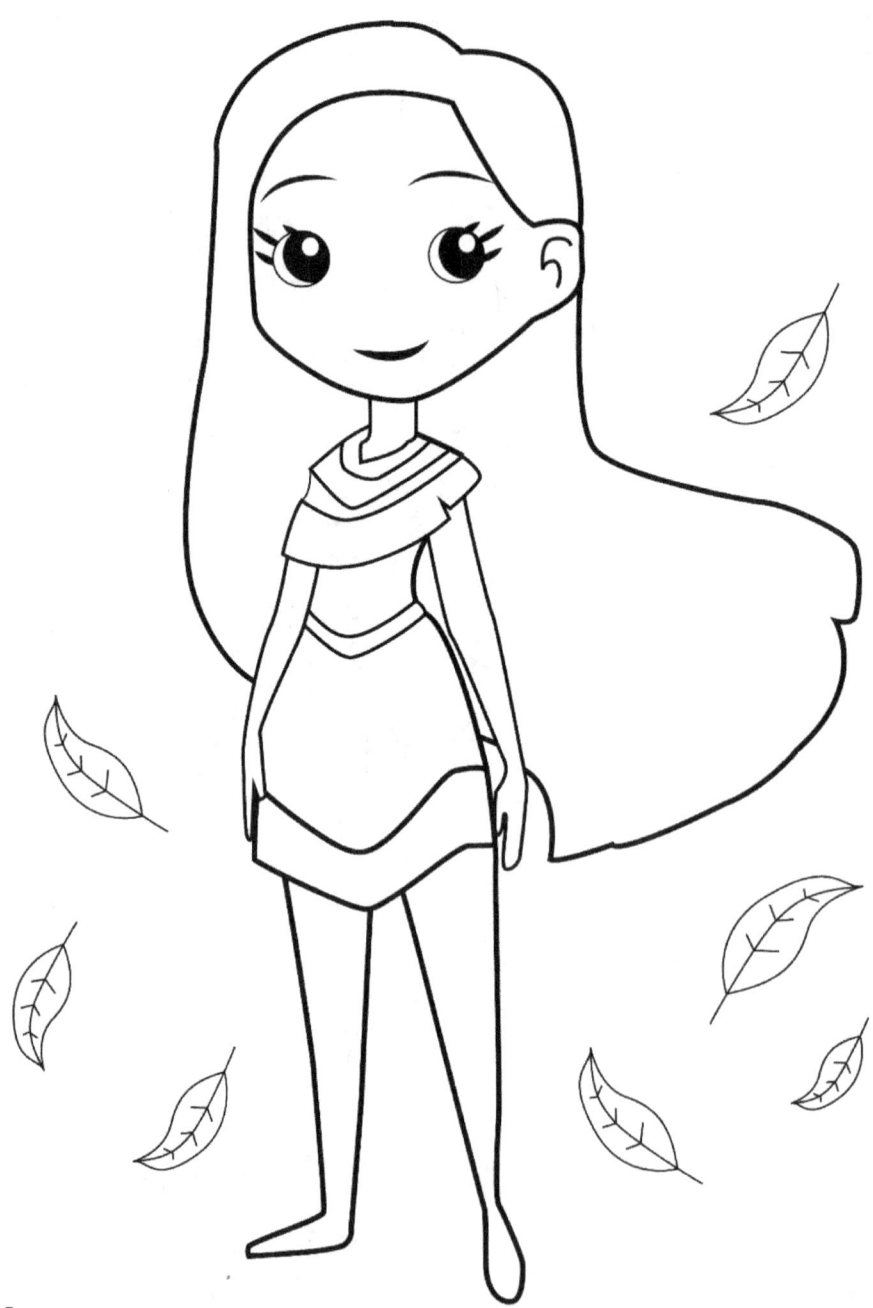

NAME:

PRINCESS

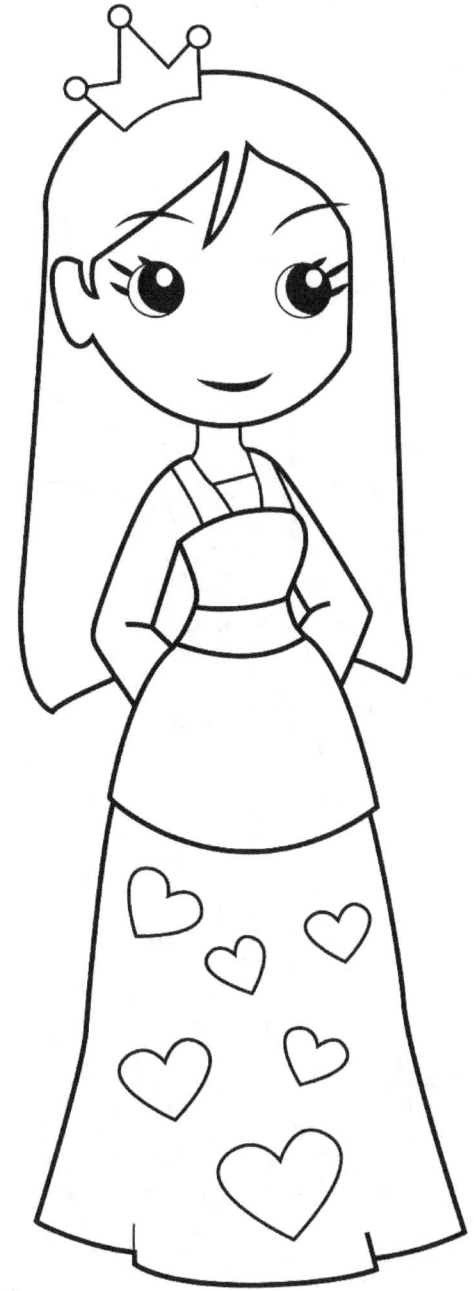

NAME:

BABY UNICORN

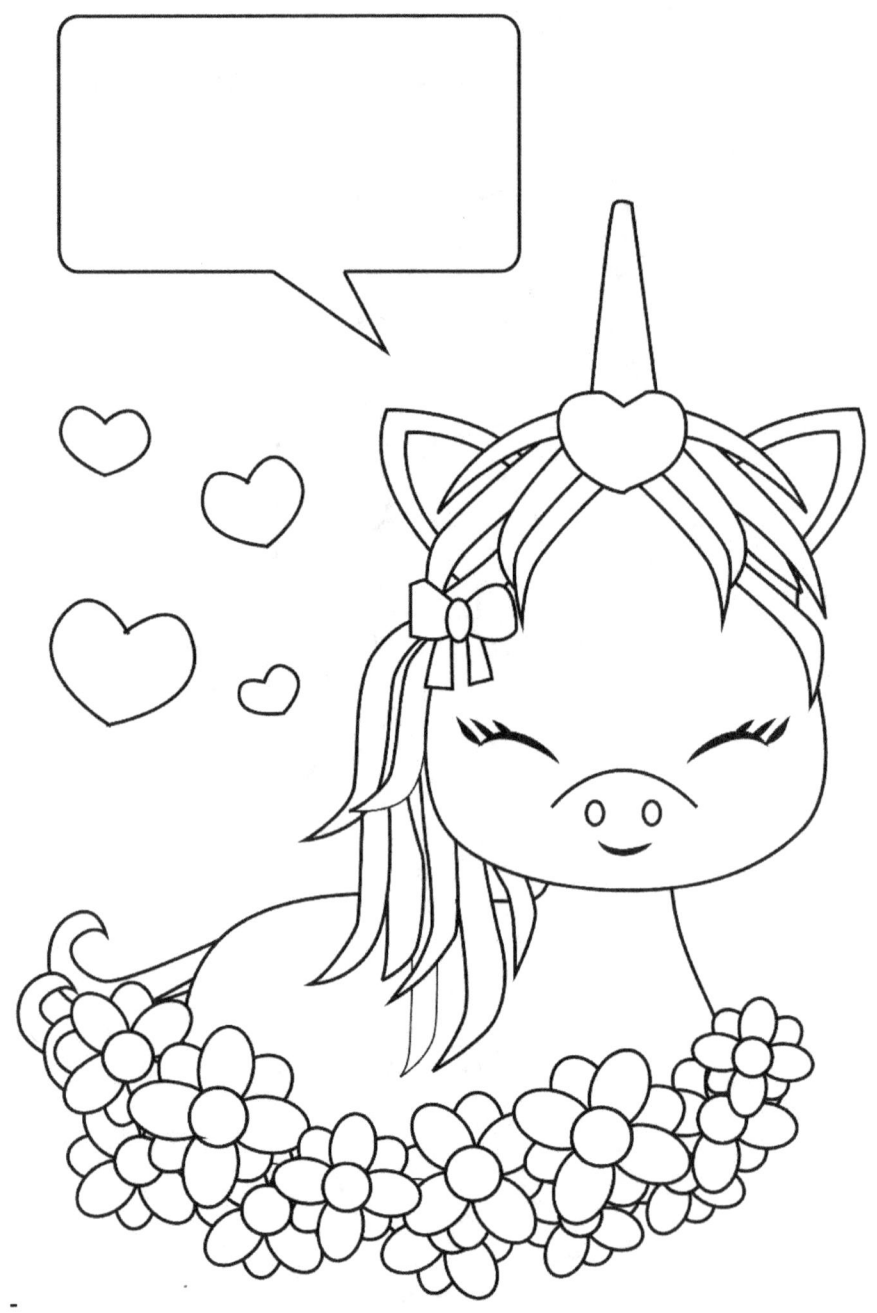

NAME:

PRINCESS WITH DOG

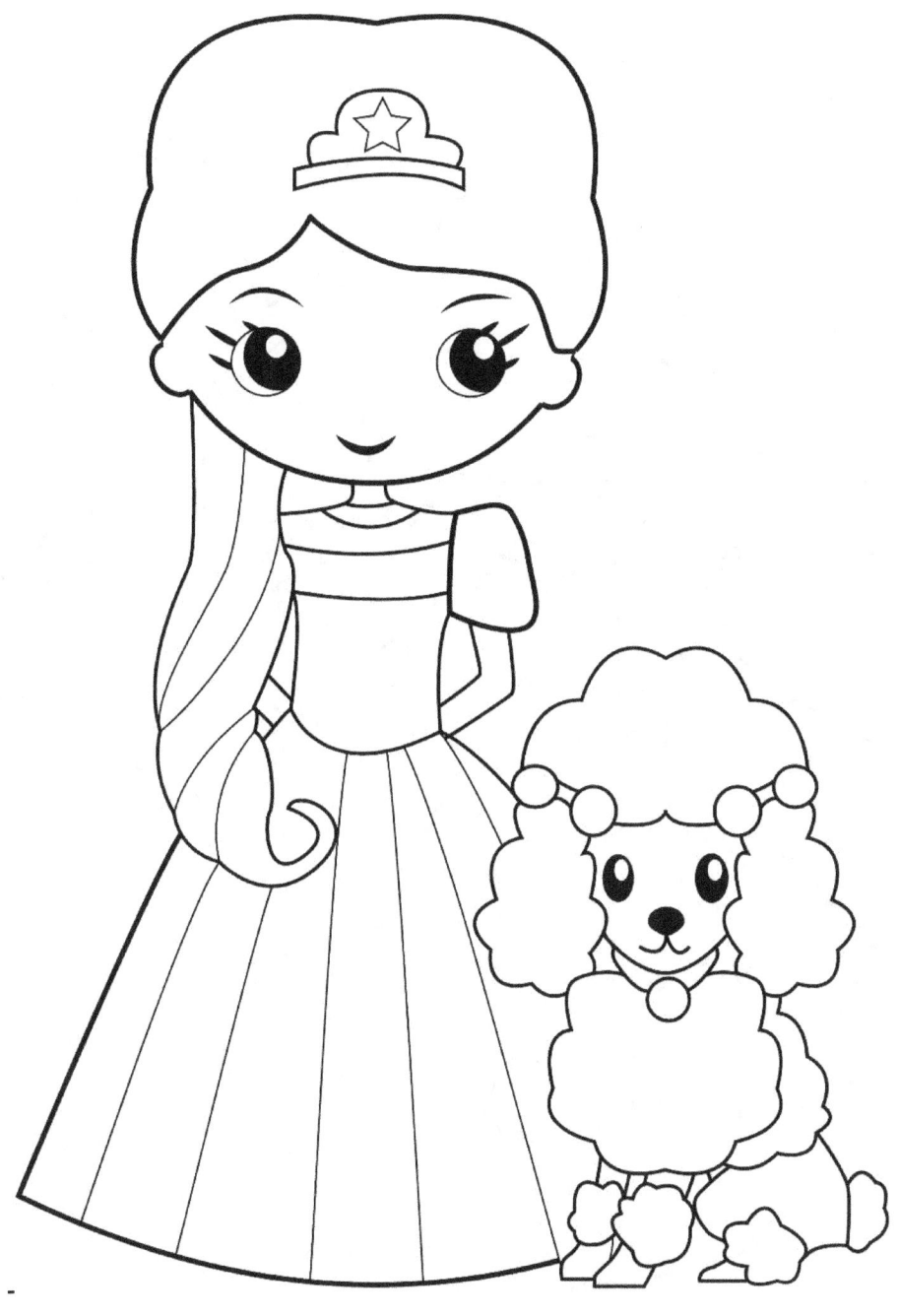

NAME:

PRINCESS WITH BIRD

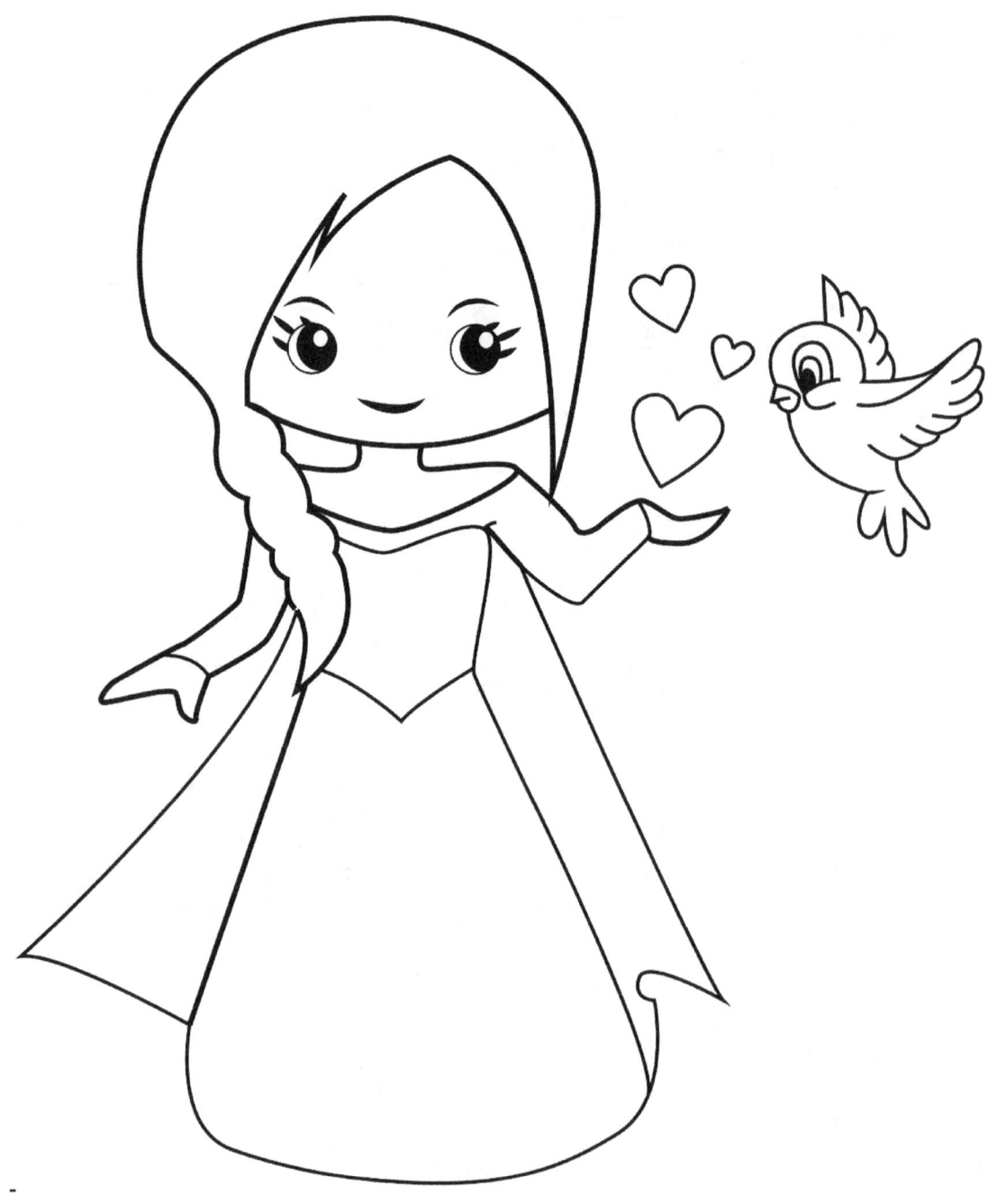

NAME:

UNICORN

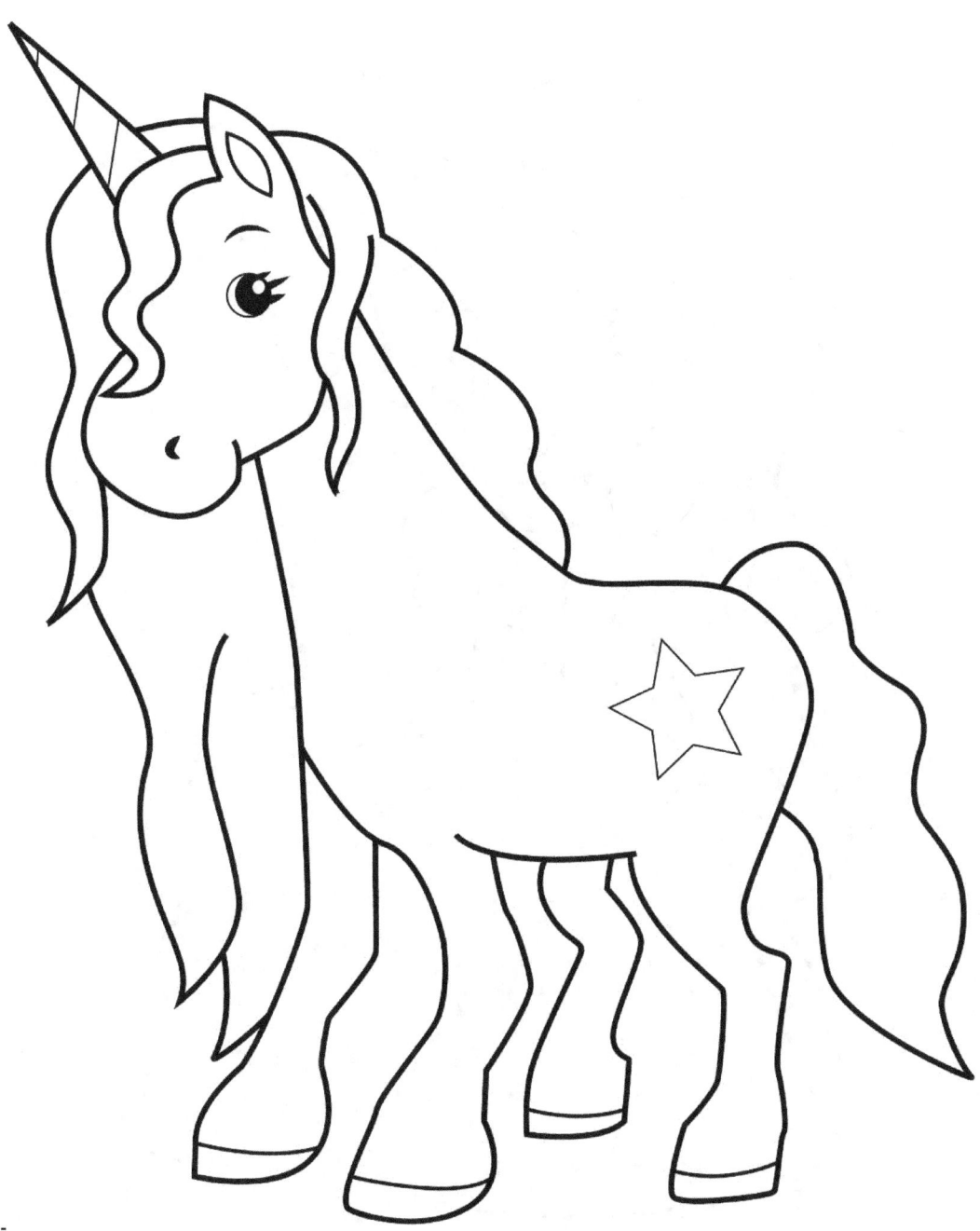

NAME:

PRINCESS

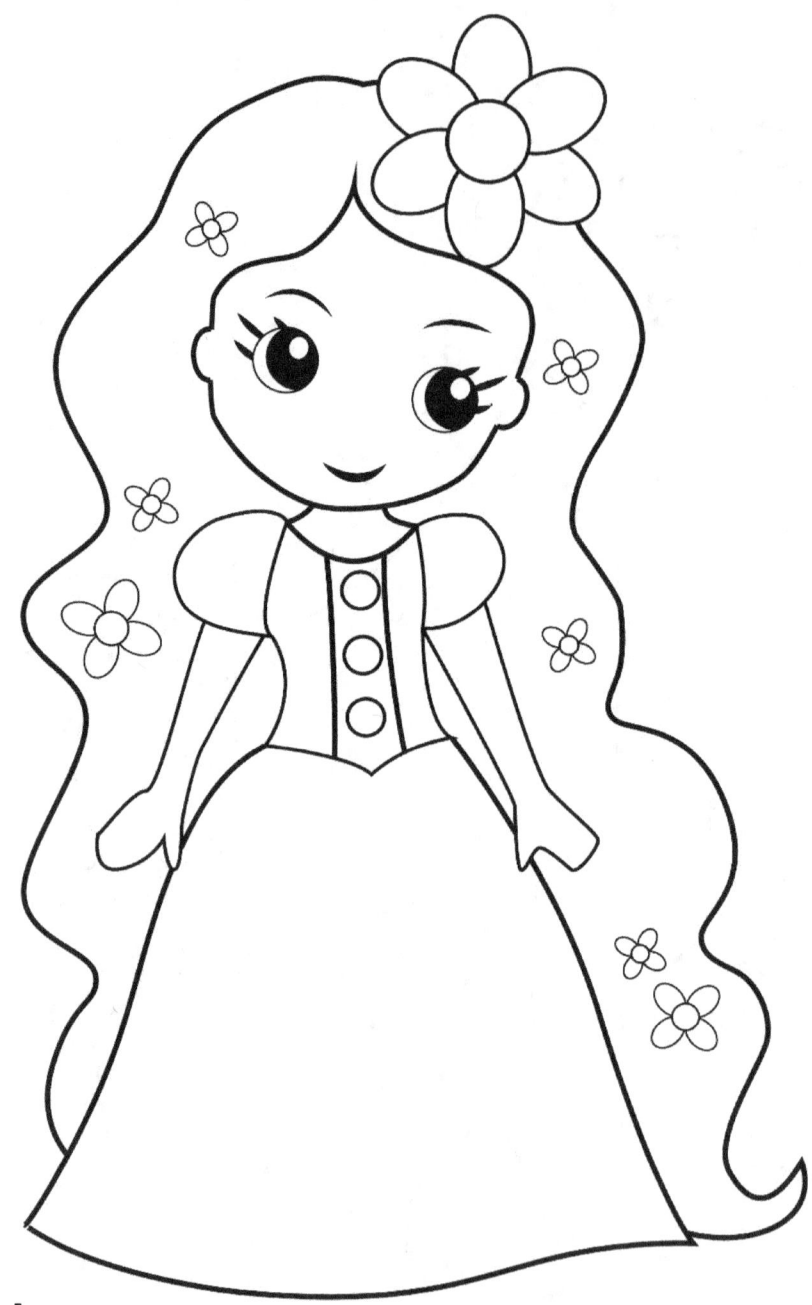

NAME:

PRINCE CAT

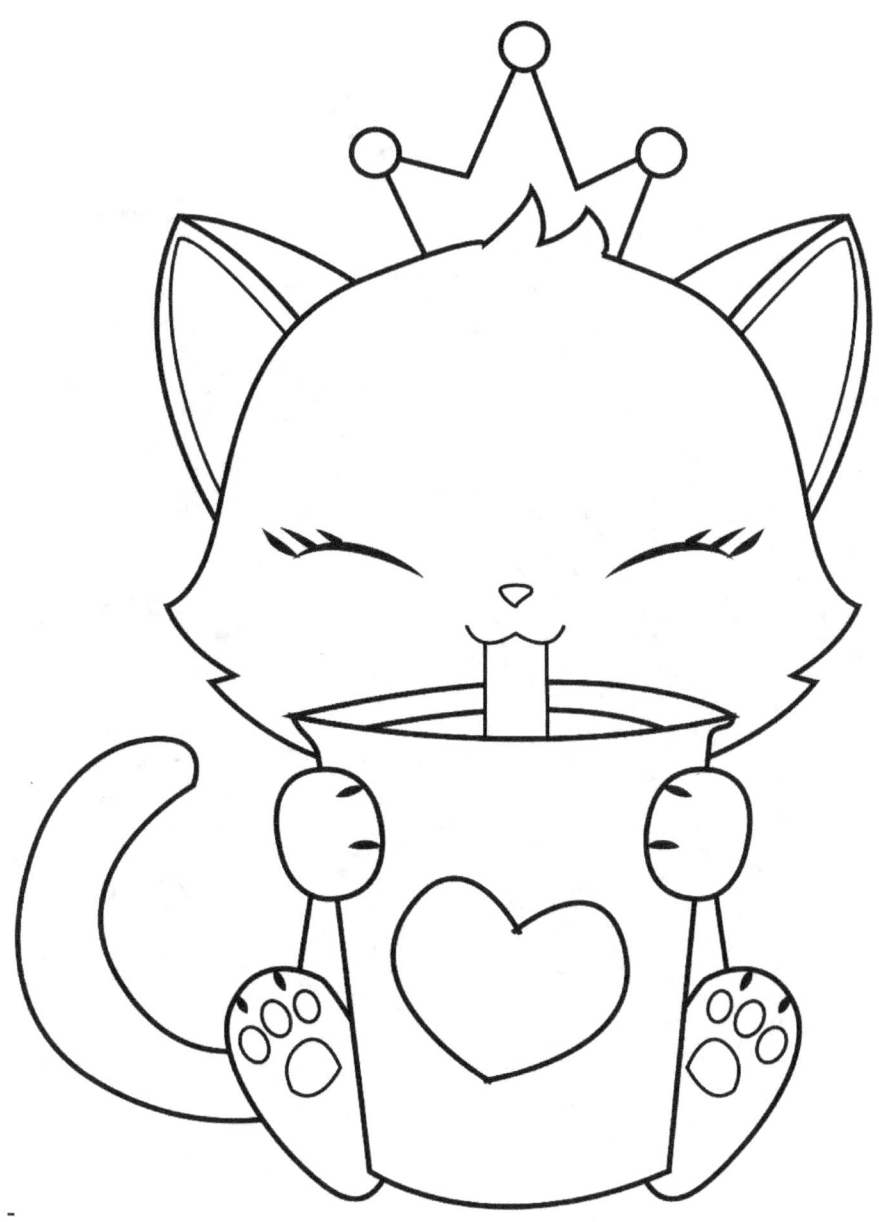

NAME:

RAINBOW

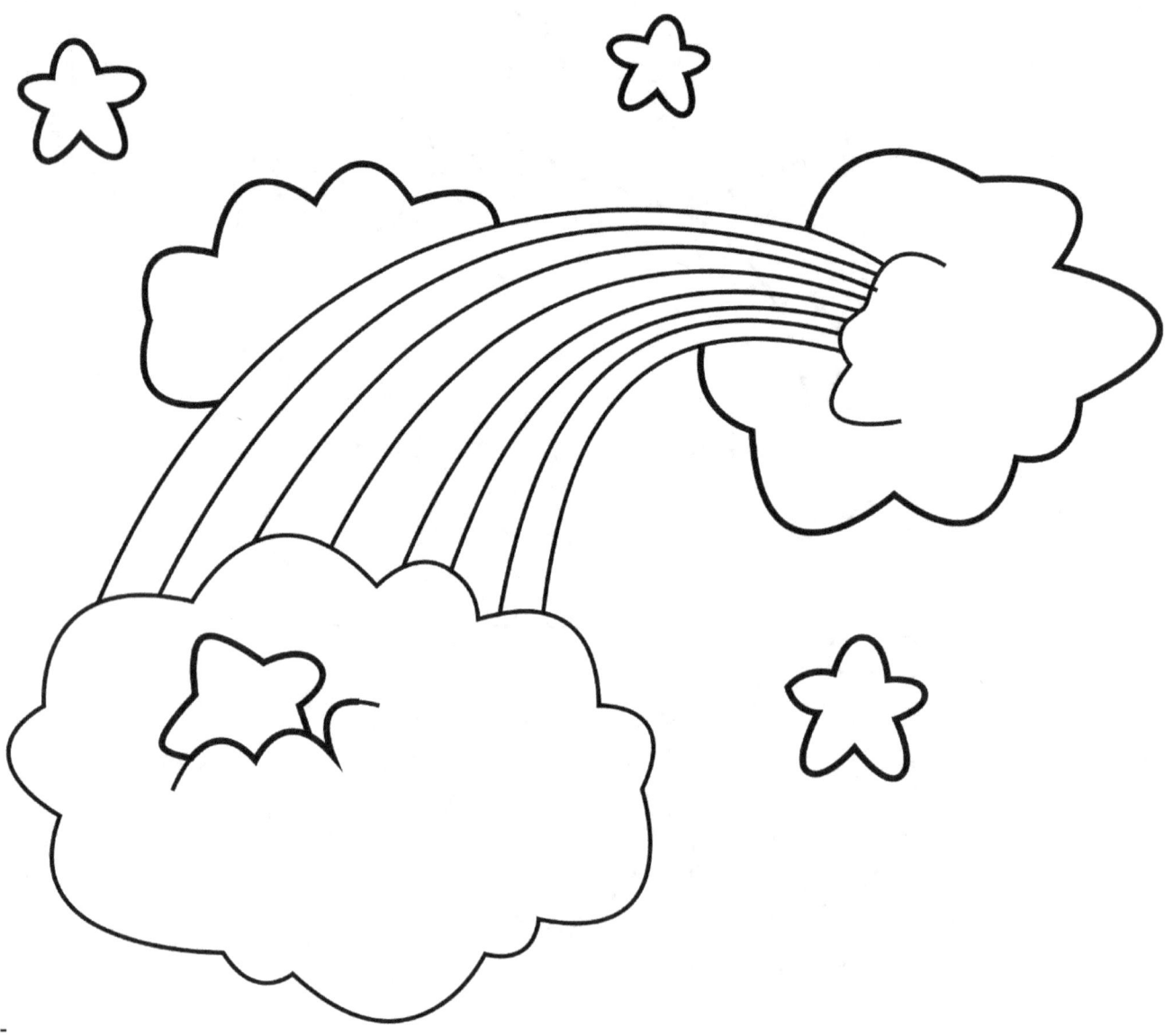

NAME:

CASTLE

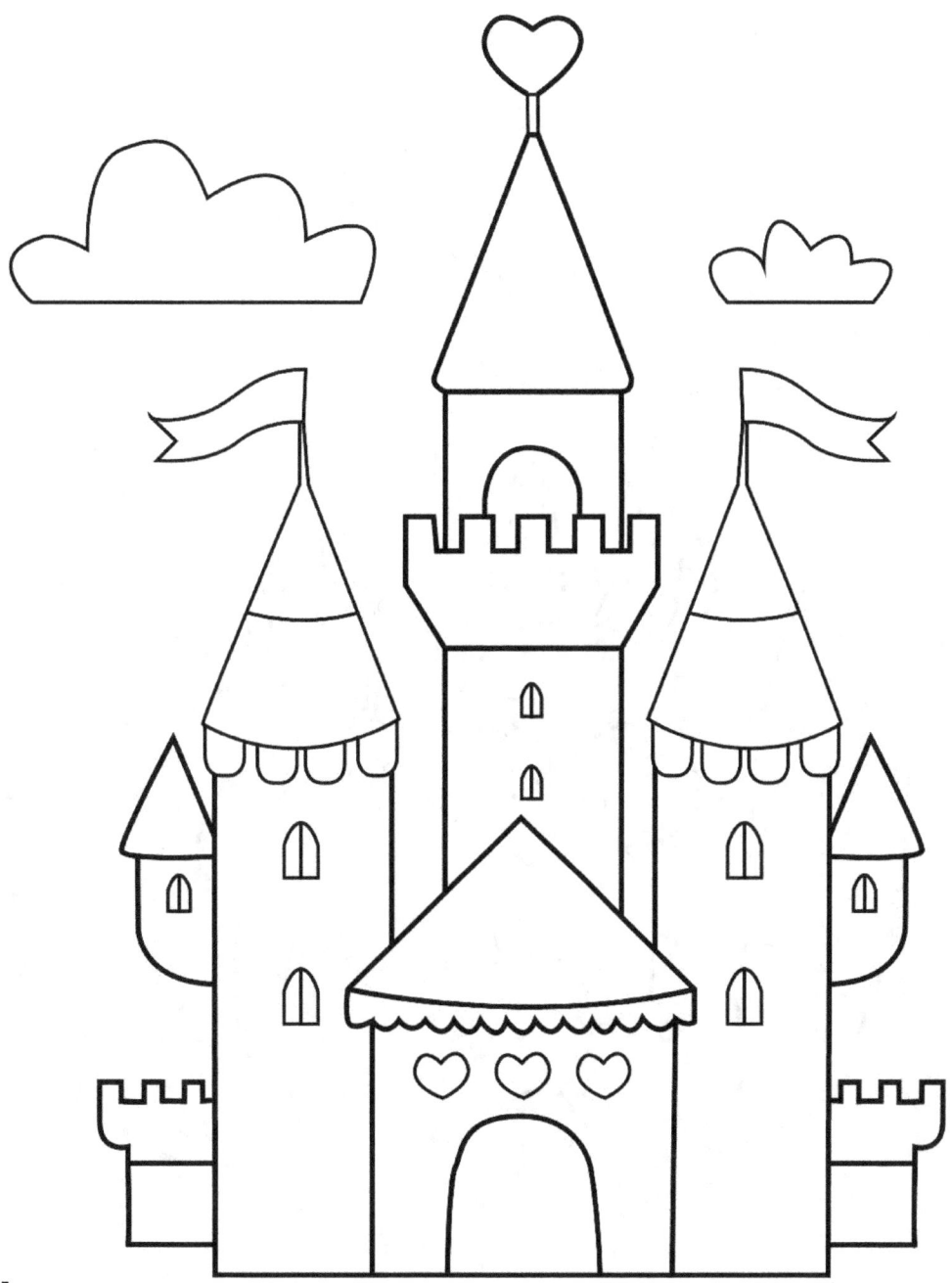

NAME:

SQUIRRELS

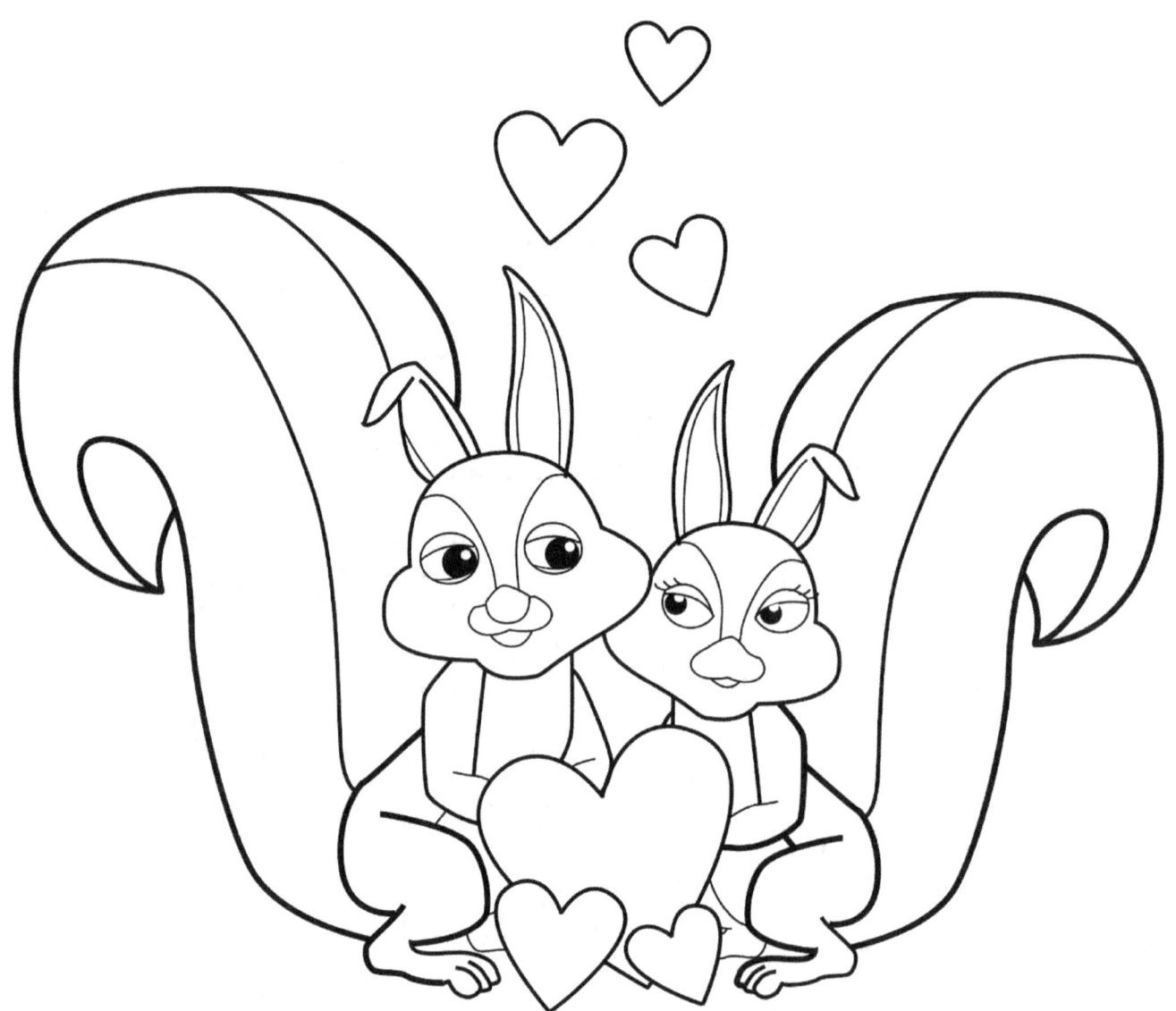

NAME:

QUEEN

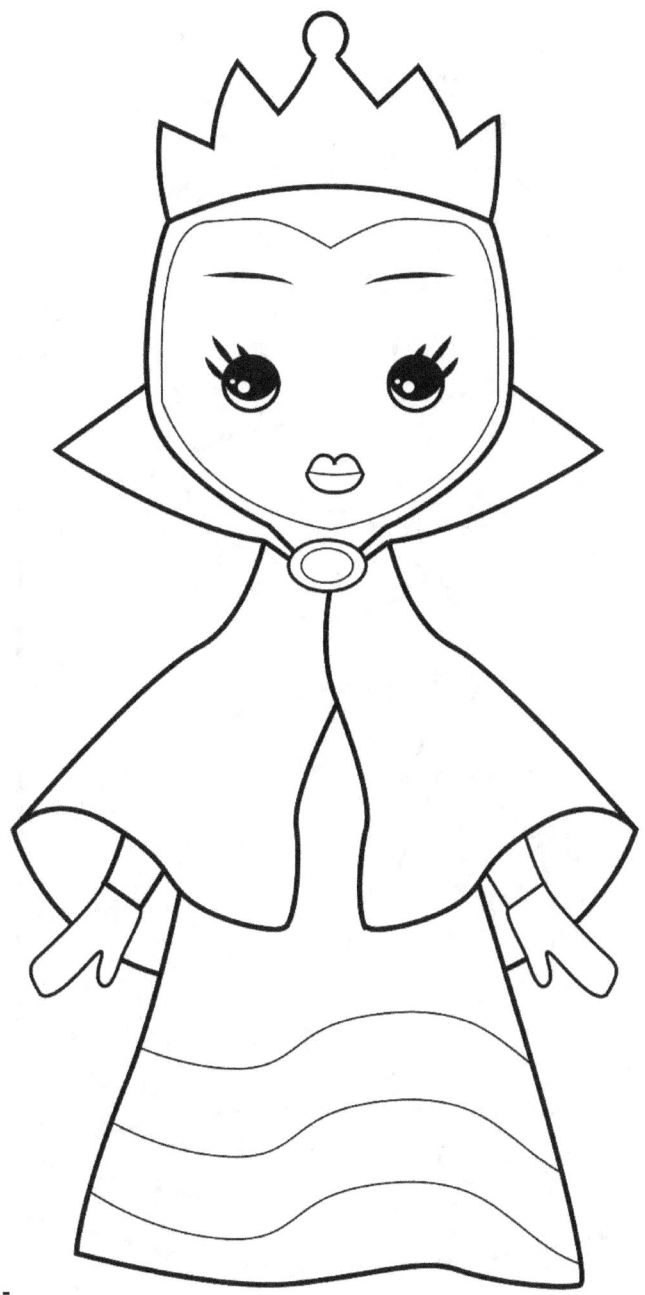

NAME:

ROSE

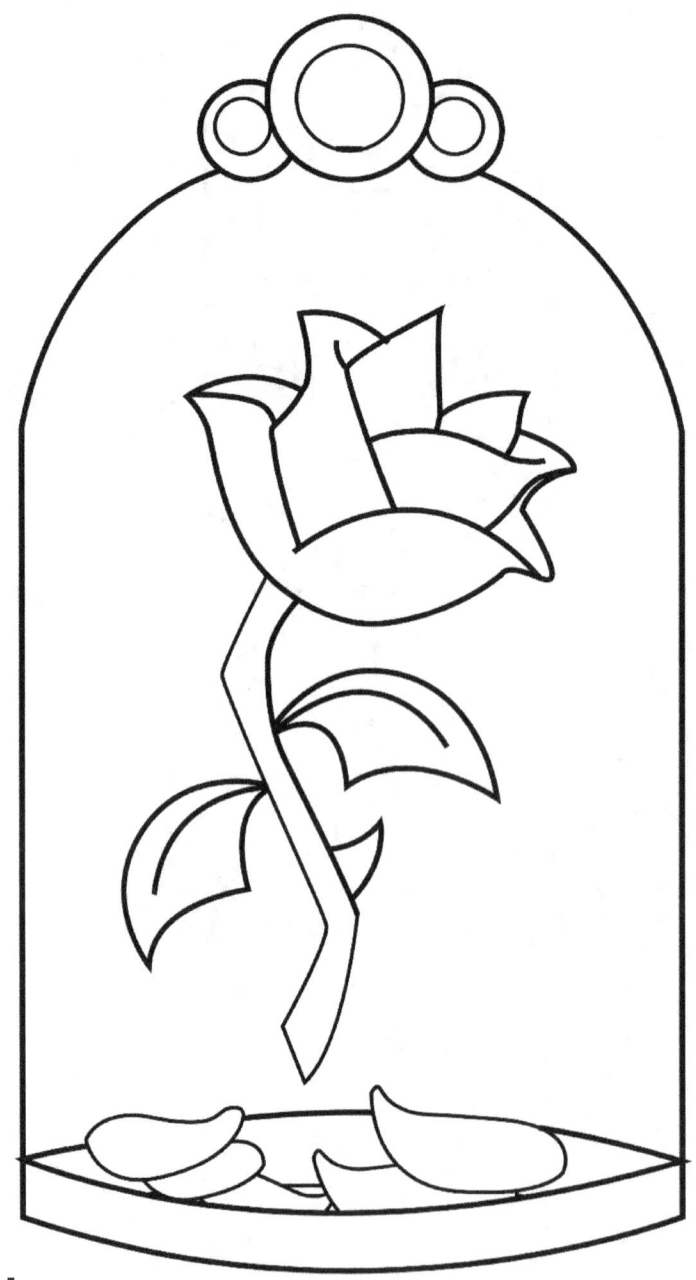

NAME:

PRINCESS

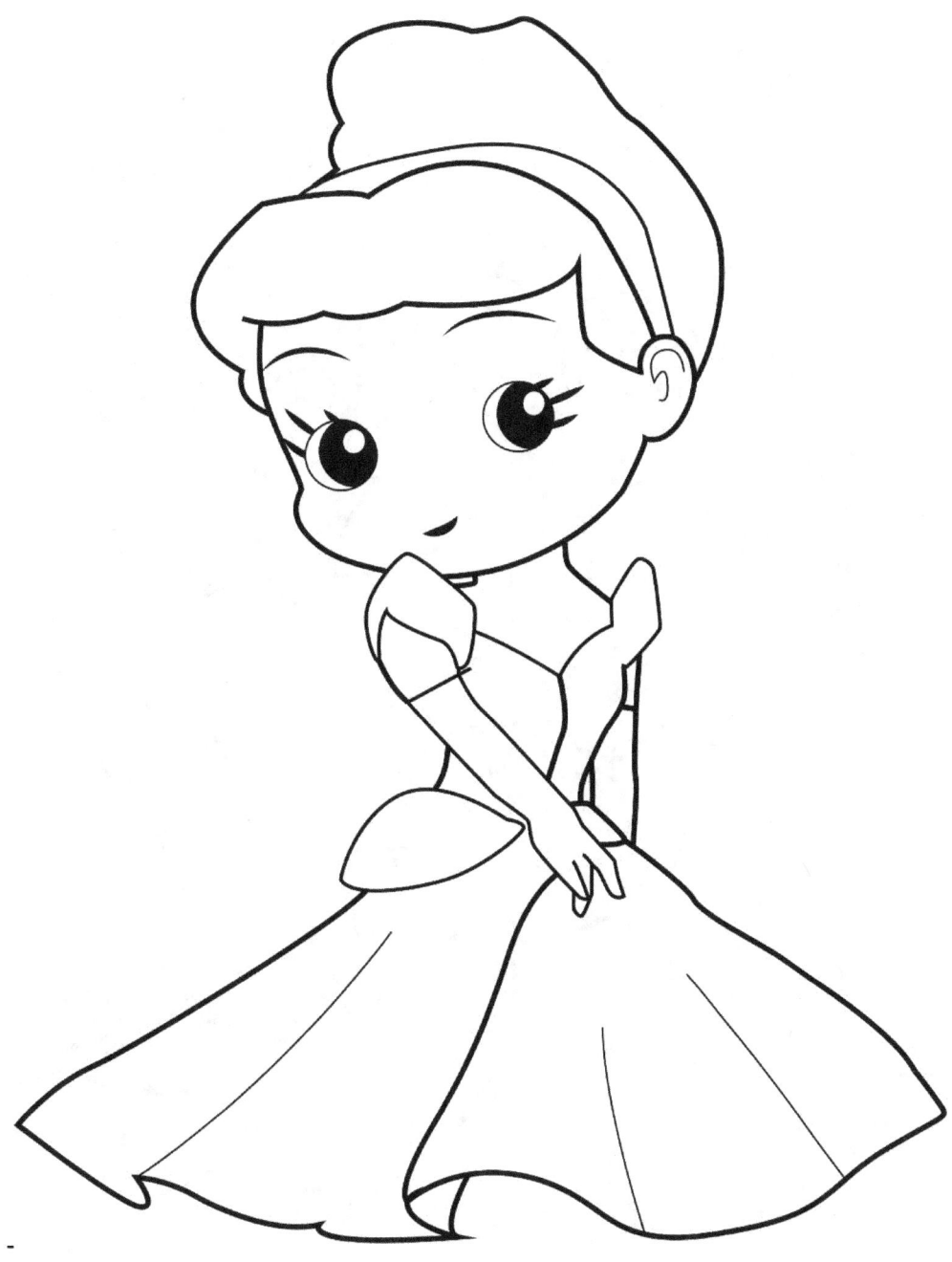

NAME:

DRAGONS

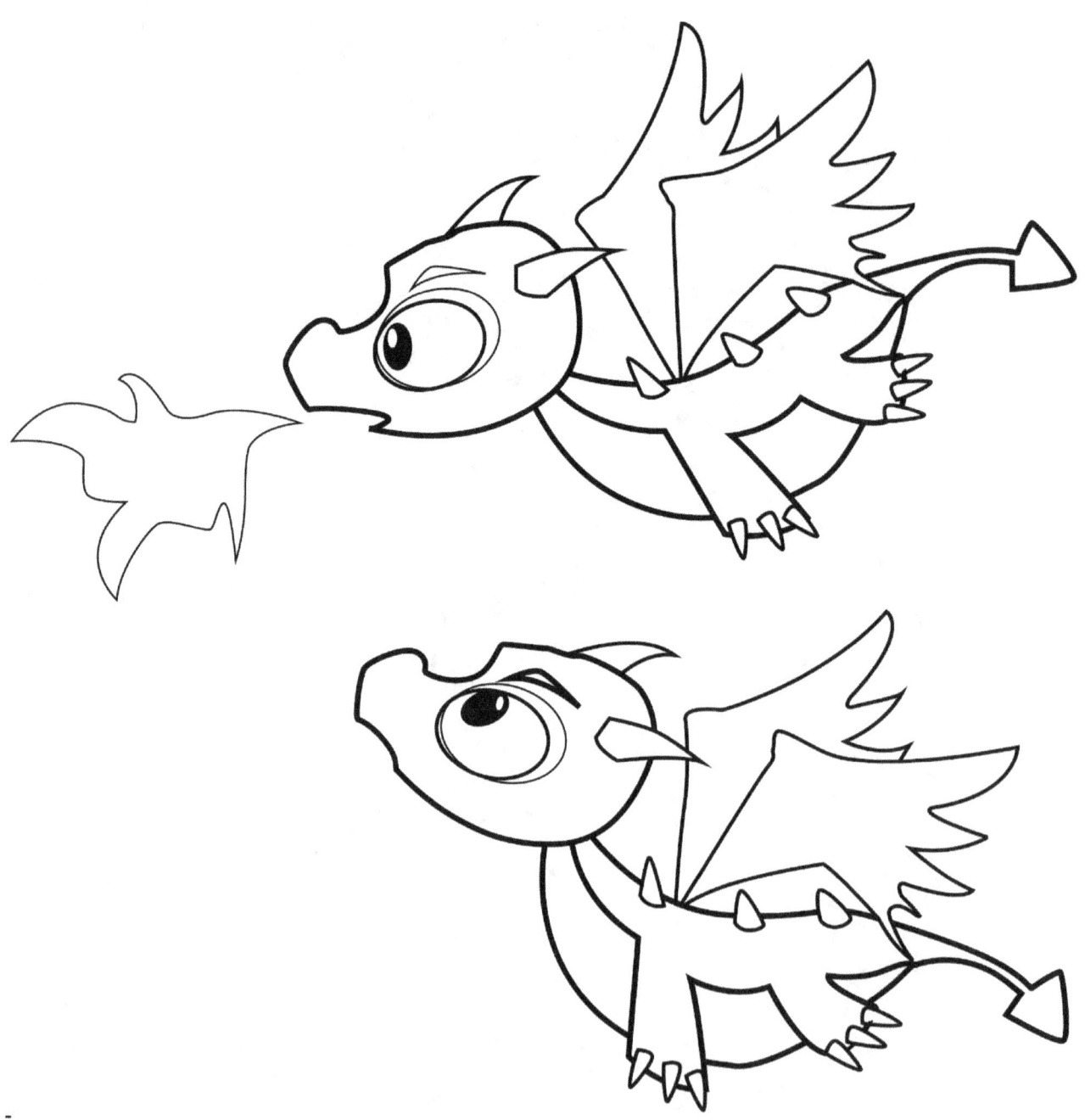

NAME:

PRINCESS

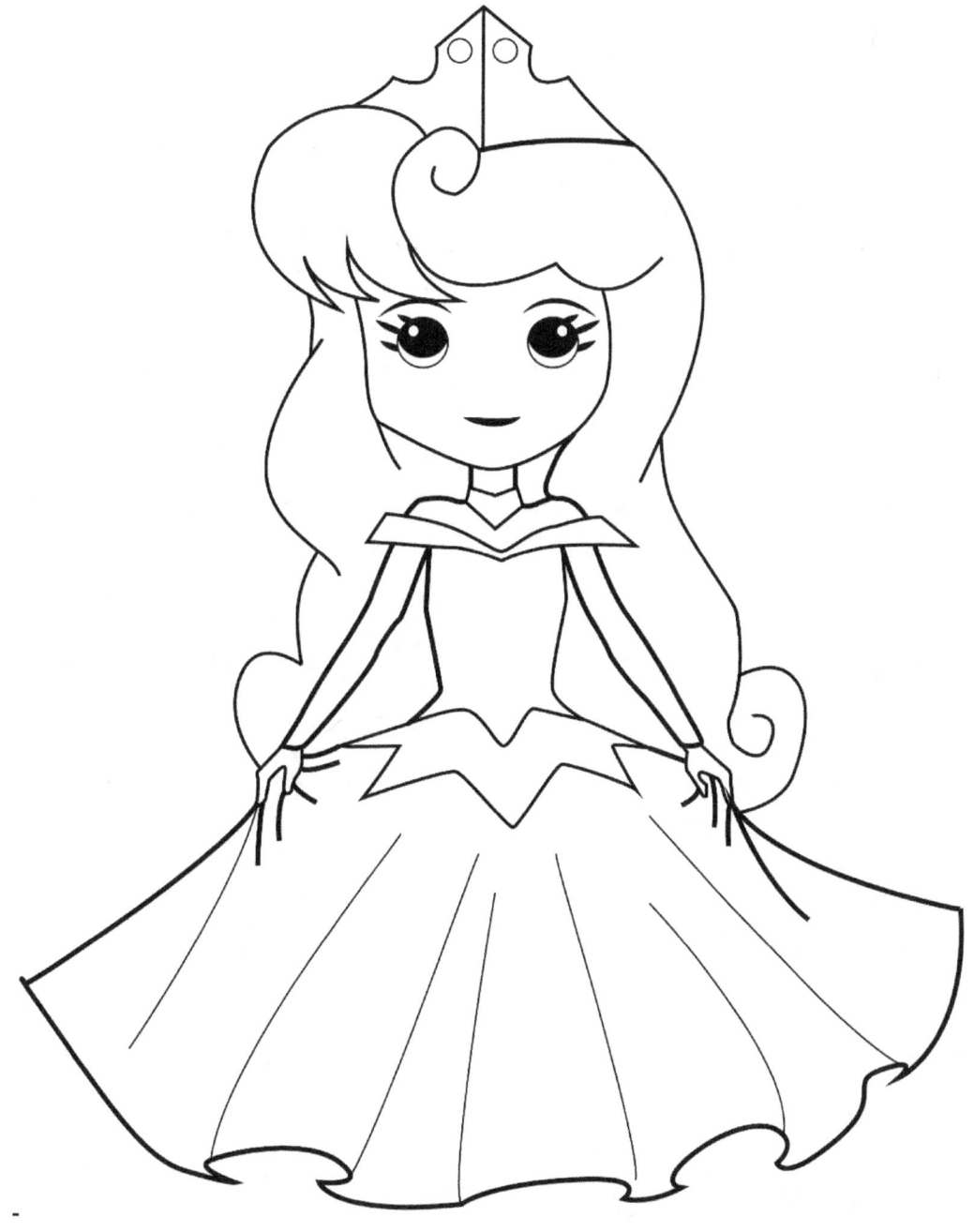

NAME:

CONCLUSION

I truly hope you and your children enjoyed this book.

Knowing that I have contributed to develop your kid's skills and fantasy is my biggest satisfaction.

To Jake and Hillary, my inspiration and my heart.

Love,
Kara

www.ingramcontent.com/pod-product-compliance
Lightning Source LLC
Chambersburg PA
CBHW080952220526
45465CB00008BA/3257